TOWARDS BICULTURAL COMPETENCE
BEYOND BLACK AND WHITE

Arvinda,   To our
" New Beginnings "
            Alma
            17.10.07

Towards Bicultural Competence
beyond black and white

Gloria Gordon

Trentham Books

Stoke on Trent, UK and Sterling, USA

Trentham Books Limited

Westview House   22883 Quicksilver Drive
734 London Road   Sterling
Oakhill   VA 20166-2012
Stoke on Trent   USA
Staffordshire
England ST4 5NP

First published 2007

British Library Cataloguing-in-Publication Data
A catalogue record for this book is available from the British Library

ISBN: 978-1-85856-397-8

Designed and typeset by Trentham Print Design Ltd, Chester and printed in Great Britain by Hobbs the Printers Ltd, Hampshire.

Contents

Figures

Insist on yourself; never imitate. Your own gift you can present every moment with the cumulative force of a whole life's cultivation; but of the adopted talent of another, you have only an extemporaneous, half possession. That which each can do best, none but his Maker can teach him. No man yet knows what it is, nor can, till that person has exhibited it. Where is the master who could have taught Shakespeare? Where is the master who could have instructed Franklin, or Washington, or Bacon, or Newton? Every great man is a unique. The Scipionism of Scipio is precisely that part he could not borrow. Shakespeare will never be made by the study of Shakespeare. Do that which is assigned you, and you cannot hope too much or dare too much. There is at this moment for you an utterance brave and grand as that of the colossal chisel of Phidias, or trowel of the Egyptians, or the pen of Moses, or Dante, but different from all these. Not possibly will the soul all rich, all eloquent, with thousand-cloven tongue, deign to repeat itself; but if you can hear what these patriarchs say, surely you can reply to them in the same pitch of voice; for the ear and the tongue are two organs of one nature. Abide in the simple and noble regions of thy life, obey thy heart, and thou shalt reproduce the Foreworld again.

(Emerson 1841/1995)

Acknowledgements

First and foremost I give thanks to my own inner teacher for guiding me through the process of this journey of authentic human inquiry and development. Secondly, my sons, Joel, Nicholas and Micah: you have been the catalysts for my embarking on this journey at all. This legacy has primarily been developed to support you on your journeys through life. And through you, all the members of our precious ethnic family, the descendants of enslaved Africans. In writing this book and sharing with you as I have done I am passing on the baton. It is a legacy for the three of you to build on and transmit down our generational chain so that once again, as the descendants of enslaved Africans, we can enter onto the world stage of life as a group.

I have also been particularly blessed by spiritual teachers whose wisdom and humanity have inspired me on my journey from unconsciousness to consciousness. Those who have made their transition include Neville, Joel and Walter. A living teacher is Oprah Winfrey.

I also thank all the individuals who over the years have blessed my life in different ways. You know who you are. Blessings have not always taken the form I would have preferred but, nevertheless, they have helped to bring me to this point. For this I am grateful.

It is appropriate to acknowledge the 2002 NTFS award and research fellowship, a life-time award and the symbolism of which I have drawn on to support me in main-taining the strength and courage to pursue the research underpinning this book thus far. I have used the award in some of my darkest hours as a sign that the ideas shared are important and that the race is won by those who can endure.

Heartfelt gratitude goes to my publisher, Gillian, and the proof-readers who have painstakingly supported me in developing what I have found so difficult to put into words. I am particularly pleased to be publishing with Trentham Books because of their dedication to working with social justice issues over the years.

Preface

This book has been an immense challenge for me to write, sharing as it does the life-changing journey of moving from unconsciousness to consciousness around the topic of race and what it means for me to be black in Britain. The challenge has been in sharing an experience which has been silenced and therefore the courage needed to break through the silence in order to surface the issues that lie behind it. Writing up the journey has been an important part of the transformation process as I have worked through ideas on paper, tested them out in daily life and returned to the laboratory of my mind and heart, subjecting them to deeper consideration. Writing a book about personal inner explorations is not something many of us do nor is it something I had contemplated as possible. That was until I realised the gravity of the black experience, the number of lives destroyed as a result and realised intuitively that the only way I was going to be able to get to the heart of the matter was to use my own life-world as the research terrain. Apart from shedding important and needed light on the black experience the journey placed me on the path to authentic human development. The process has revealed that the very thing I was most afraid of was what I had to learn to walk through to become free within myself. When I started the research I was seeking to create a legacy for young black people in British society. On completion of the book I believe that as a result of working through the silenced experience of the descendants of enslaved Africans I have made a contribution to furthering humanity.

In sharing the process of giving birth to a new way of being I hope to inspire other descendants of enslaved Africans to do the work of walking through our life experiences because this is the path to ending psychological slavery. It is also the path to healing damaged lives and relationships. What emerges from my journey is a new British African-Caribbean perspective, shedding light into the darkness and moving us beyond black and white cultures to surface our own authentic folk cultures. The book represents a challenge to the silences we keep, the knowledge and histories we hide, deny and repress, the peoples and cultures we blame, including our children, when we should be looking to ourselves: the reasons for our failures lie within ourselves and not outside.

The fact that I am now a life in conscious process is apparent from the above. The book reveals that most of my life lacked authenticity and personal integrity as I existed in a survival mode in British culture and society. Most of my energies were expended in imitating and accommodating the ethnic majority in order to survive. This was the dysfunctional culture I was transmitting to my own children. I have only now arrived at the point where I understand my life experiences well enough to begin to take on the challenges of living as a whole human being.

Writing this book has primarily been about engaging with the struggle to find my own authentic voice as well as developing the courage to break through the silence of the culture to speak as the descendant of enslaved Africans. It has been critical for me to gain a transcendent overview of the issues, enabling me to put the black and white experiences in perspective so that members of the two groups can move beyond our current oppositional yet symbiotic relationship. The critical nature of this endeavour comes from the fact that descendants of enslaved Africans still don't have access to each other as members of a functioning community because our relationships continue to be mediated by the authority of the ethnic majority. Where there are signs of struggles, inconsistencies, contradictions and hesitations affecting the text they should be understood in the spirit of my giving birth to something new, which is radically different from what has existed before.

The poignancy of this book being published in the year of the 200th anniversary of the abolition of the slave trade is also acknowledged. It is a year in which slavery is more in the media than ever before with the black community uniting in making demands for slavery to be taught as part of the official curriculum for all children in Britain.

1

Introduction

The black man or woman who is born here and grows up here has something special to contribute to western civilisations. He or she will participate in it, see it from birth, but will never be quite completely in it. What such persons have to say, therefore, will give a new vision, a deeper and stronger insight into both western civilisation and the black people in it. (C L R James, 1984)

You are a human being ... and so you have a philosophical view of existence – whether you realise it or not. About this you have no choice. But there is a choice to be made about your philosophy and it can be put in these terms: is your philosophy based on conscious, thoughtful and well-informed reflection? Is it sensitive to, but not chained by, the need for logical consistency? Or have you let your subconscious amass an ugly pile of unexamined prejudices, unjustified intolerances, hidden fears, doubts and implicit contradictions, thrown together by chance but integrated by your own subconscious into a kind of mongrel philosophy and fused into a single, solid weight, like a ball and chain in the place where your mind's wings should have grown? It is not the answer that enlightens but the question. (Eugene Ionescu, cited by Alchin, 2003)

I have written this book for both teachers and parents – for those of us charged with the responsibility of caring for and preparing new generations for life and living. Erikson (1950) referred to this quality of care as 'generativity': an interest in establishing and guiding the next generation. The idea of generativity extends beyond biological procreation to include productivity, creativity and caring for one's sector of the world, seen in his view that the perpetuation of mankind challenges the generative ingenuity of workers and thinkers of many kinds. Kotre (1983) extends Erikson's thinking when he defines generativity as a desire to invest one's substance in forms of life and work that will outlive the self. Kotre suggests four types of generativity:

- Biological – having children

- Parental – nurturing children into family traditions

- Technical – teaching skills through passing on the 'content' of a culture

- Cultural – creating, renovating and conserving a symbol system

This typology helps us to understand that as educators we are engaged in different types and levels of activity that can be generative or non-generative. Although as a parent and educator I am involved in all four types I have not always been consciously aware of them. Certainly I sometimes lacked confidence in fulfilling the obligations of parental and technical generativity and was especially conflicted about the technical generativity of my educational practice in higher education. Despite my desire to transmit a positive generative legacy I suspected that, without realising it, I was actively engaged in transmitting dysfunctional non-generative legacies. This doubt led me to research what it means for me to be black in Britain, this being the most problematic aspect of my life experience. Fullan's (1993) assertion that teaching is fundamentally a moral profession, requiring educators to be agents of change, supported my concerns. He writes about how trainee teachers enter the profession because they want '... to make a difference' but are then faced by the inevitable difficulties of teaching and lose their way when

> ... desire interacts with personal issues and vulnerabilities, as well as social pressures and values, to engender a sense of frustration and force a reassessment of the possibilities of the job and the investment one wants to make to it.

Such frustration is engendered through our failure to realise that this very trouble-some experience is what we entered the profession to make a difference with. Attending to personal issues and vulnerabilities as they meet with social pressures and values is how we can role-model to our students how to attend to the inevitable challenges which life will also confront them with. Gorringe (2004) uses the analogy of nature when he makes reference to the necessity of us 'cultivating' the human soil of our life through learning what is possible and what is not, as we respond to local conditions of soil and climate. In the process we learn to irrigate the human soil of our lives in ways which do not cause erosion or problems for our neighbour downstream.

Exploring what it means for me to be black in Britain meant I realised that I was actually engaged in transmitting the content of a culture into which I have been unconsciously assimilated. Conflicts experienced in my educational practice were the consequence of the contradictions of transmitting the official body of a culture that did not represent the reality of my experiences but was in many ways in direct opposition to it. However to teach from my centre would be to teach against the dominant culture so instead I internalised the idea that I was the problem. This left me with feelings of in-authenticity and a lack of personal integrity so that an existential crisis of meaning inevitably ensued. The race taboo (Frankenberg, 1993; Thomas, 1989) worked to prevent me from exploring my own life experiences as I con-formed to it. Because I was unable to freely attend to the human soil of my life as an educator I could not effectively facilitate others to attend to the human soil of their lives.

Audience and purpose

I write with two primary audiences in mind: formal educators in the educa-tion system and the descendants of enslaved Africans (DoEAs). However, this does not mean that the book is not relevant to a wider audience since it speaks to the human condition. At the outset of the research my main pur-pose was twofold: first, to understand the black experience which enabled me to improve the quality of my own educational practice because of the ways in which race and skin-colour impacts negatively on it. Second, to satisfy my generative desire to create a functional legacy for black learners in higher education. As the research progressed it became apparent that I was carrying out a British cultural analysis which was necessary to understanding the black experience. Ultimately, I was to learn about what it means for me to be a human being. Palmer (1997) makes the point well when he acknowledges:

> Good teaching depends less on technique than it does on the human condition of the teacher, and only by knowing the truth of our own condition can we hope to know the true condition of our students.

In particular I share:

- the significance of educators engaging in human inquiry and, there-fore, a journey similar to my own necessary for authentic human development (ie the journey from unconsciousness to conscious-ness)

- the value and importance of approaching our educational practice as cultural workers because of the responsibilities inherent in the role

- the importance of all educators understanding race and the black and white experiences because of how it impacts on all our lives and classroom practice

- the personal vision-building capacity that results from making the choice for authenticity and integrity

3

These four contributions were critical to my gaining a National Teaching Fellowship Scheme (NTFS) Award and Research Fellowship in 2002 for demonstrating excellence in teaching and learning. Excellence in my case is the outcome of adopting an experiential, personal and collaborative action research and inquiry approach to life, resulting in my engagement with human inquiry as a life-long pursuit.

Background to the research

The background to my decision to engage in research to develop my educational practice is the outcome of finding myself in a society and higher education institution where silence surrounds the black experience and, therefore, me. The inherent sense of threat that results from this silence became a significant blocking mechanism for me. Francis and Woodcock (1996) define a blockage as 'a factor which inhibits the potential and output of a system'. They argue for finding those things that are holding you back, overcoming negative feelings and removing the blockage. The decision to engage with what it means to be black in Britain was to result in the development of important insights into how race acts as a significant blockage in the black experience. In working to understand and remove the blockage I made the choice for:

▦ Teacher authenticity and integrity

My crisis of meaning resulted from the experience of meaninglessness in my life as a black British member of this society. Forced to accommodate the ethnic majority to protect my livelihood I lacked authenticity and personal integrity. Not least was the realisation that this crisis was somehow linked to my heritage as the DoEA, and the silence that surrounds this experience was central to the crisis. My inner desire was to be real and to find congruence between external and internal realities. Silence could no longer be a part of my everyday experience.

▦ Understanding race and silence

My MBA research (Bravette, 1993) revealed silence not only as a significant societal issue but more importantly I was shown to have internalised it. I resolved to penetrate the silence and the blockage it created in my inner world because of the consequences for my life and educational practice. This made me realise that issues such as social inequality are not distinct and separate from the classroom but are an integral component of the teaching and learning process and must be addressed in our classrooms. As teachers we are role models and students are learning from us even what we do not intend to teach: the silences we keep around important social issues are being taught to our learners. Although the race taboo was damaging to me I was complicit in maintaining it. Realising that I was an ineffective role model, I sought to transform my own experiences because in satisfying the stereotype of what it means to be black I was perpetuating social inequality along the lines of race. Failed attempts to get institutional agents to respond to these issues as I raised them eventually led me to adopt Gandhi's (2007) call to be the change I want to see. This decision anchored my own call to respond to race as an issue as it negatively impacted on my life. Whereas British culture called me as a descendent of enslaved Africans (DoEA) to tokenism my spirit, my inner life, was calling me to self-expression. This meant removing the blockage of race and silence from my life.

Matsuura (2004) acknowledges that unlike other human tragedies, such as the Jewish holocaust, the silence surrounding the tragedy of slavery and its consequences is deafening. In seeking to interrupt the silence 2004 was elected as the international year for the commemoration of slavery. Matsuura stated that:

> By institutionalising memory, resisting the onset of oblivion, recalling the memory of a tragedy that for long years remained hidden or unrecognised and by assigning it its proper place in the human conscience we respond to our duty to remember. To that end, we must promote the history of the slave trade and slavery and make it known to the general public: we must also devote ourselves to rigorous scientific research that highlights the whole historical truth about the tragedy in a constructive perspective. As a matter of urgency this major episode in the history of humanity, whose consequences are permanently imprinted in the world's geography and economy, should take its full place in the school textbooks and curricula of every country in the world.

Fiona MacTaggart (2004) made the following official response to Matsuura's call:

> ... slavery and the slave trade represent a tragic chapter in the history of the world and one of the worst examples of man's inhumanity to man. But it cannot simply be ... consigned to the past – the legacies of slavery are all around us through the profound impact it has had on shaping the world today ... There is a duty on us all to remember, understand and apply the lessons of these legacies to the future so that we build a world where tolerance, equality and diversity are celebrated.

Thus we recognise the call for the race taboo and the silence to be violated through remembrance. These sentiments resonated with my own concerns about the impact slavery continued to have on my life experience in contemporary society. Consequently, this ongoing research contributes to the project of institutionalising the memory of slavery for the DoEAs because I now understand that we must fly this particular flag for freedom. My work also responds to Matsuura's timely call for research on the interactions at the micro-level between blacks and whites to ascertain the impact of slavery on them.

■ Understanding myself as a cultural worker

The decision to work through social issues as they impacted on my educational practice clarified the idea of creating culture as the human task. This idea is underscored by the current demand from government for teachers not only to teach 'British values' but to become lifelong learners. This is a timely call because it is an opportunity to reflect on precisely what these British values are and to explore the gap between what we espouse in theory and what we live out in practice. Our fundamental responsibility as educators is to facilitate students to become effective creators of culture or designs for living in their own right. Such cultures need to be responsive to human needs as we meet the challenges of life in a rapidly changing and increasingly globalised world. These demands suggest that as educators we should be conscious creators of culture ourselves. I could not fulfil the demands of this role effectively since I was trapped in unconsciousness on so many levels.

This understanding that the human task was to be conscious creators of culture was to become the underlying theme of my entire research (Bravette, 1997) as I pursued the concept of culture as holding the answers to my crisis. This was to culminate in the development of the bicultural competence matrix which underpins much of my work. The basic thesis of the bicultural argument, borrowed from minority scholars, is that ethnic minority people living in plural societies should undergo socialisation into two cultures: a culture of origin and a culture of residence (DeAnda, 1984). The matrix consists of four quadrants vying between consciousness versus unconsciousness and competence versus incompetence. The ultimate goal is both consciousness and competence (bottom right quadrant).

Figure 1.1: Bicultural Competence Matrix

	Unconscious	Conscious
Bicultural Incompetence	*don't know I don't know* Remedy: Nurturing	*know I don't know* Remedy: Self-re-education
Bicultural Competence	*don't know I know* Remedy: needs waking from sleep	*know I know* Remedy: Maintain awareness/choice

On conceptualising the matrix I was to make the false start of assuming that African and Caribbean cultures were the missing links in my life which had resulted in my unconsciousness. This was before realising that it was the culture within which I lived, British culture, which held the key to the answers I was seeking. I pursued this idea on the premise that to gain insights into the life-world of the individual at the micro-level is to gain important insights into the life-world of the group at the macro-level. Schafer (2000) asserts:

> ... if people want to learn more about culture, cultures and their own culture in the comprehensive and all-encompassing sense, they should start with their own particular part of the whole. This could be their job, life, or geographical location in the world. But it is their job, life, or geographical location in the world, not considered in isolation, but rather as part of the larger fabric of culture as a whole. In other words, it is the details of their own specific experiences considered in terms of the larger context or container within which these experiences are situated. To progress further in this area, it is useful to focus on entities and institutions that function as wholes, and therefore have a great deal to pass on with respect to how culture and cultures function in the holistic sense.

Researching at the micro-level of my own life while working in a higher education institution has allowed me such an opportunity. In fact I got more than I bargained for as the relationship between black and white cultures was revealed. I came to understand that organisations are not rational neutral bodies but living and breathing microcosms of the societies that house them and the people who inhabit them. They operate as structures which humans impose on human interaction (Rao and Kelleher, 2000). Institutions are designed to reinforce social relations not to transform them. This was confirmed when despite my most ardent attempts I found myself confined to a 'black space'. I began to understand the university as a social location defined by a particular social vision in relation to the wider systems of social, economic and cultural relations of power, especially as this relates to what it means to be black and white.

■ Authentic human development

Making the decision to engage with my life through attending to the issues life presented me, as opposed to colluding with British culture in avoiding, repressing and fearing them, met my need for personal integrity. This put me on the path to authentic human development and the creation of my own authentic project of being (Park, 1999). My research journey and its processes made me fit for the purpose of teaching as well as yielding an answer to the problem of race which has the potential to transform lives. Emerson (1995) reveals the purpose of life when he says:

There is a time in every man's education when he arrives at the conviction that envy is ignorance; that imitation is suicide; that he must take himself for better or for worse as his portion; that though the wide universe is full of good, no kernel of nourishing corn can come to him but through his toil bestowed on that plot of ground which is given to him to till. The power which resides in him is new in nature and none but he knows what that is which he can do, nor does he know until he has tried. Not for nothing one face, one character, one fact makes much impression on him and another none. This sculpture in the memory is not without pre-established harmony. The eye was placed where one ray should fall, that it might testify of that particular ray. We but half express ourselves, and are ashamed of that divine idea which each of us represents.

My life experience as a DoEA living in Britain is the plot of ground which is given to me to till. To this point it has been hidden behind the silence of the race taboo, leaving me unexpressed and imitating the white world which dominated my black world.

In making the decision to move towards self-expression I weave together the personal with the public, the inner with the outer in crystallising the details of these four themes plus much more than I realised I needed to know. I had unwittingly stepped out into the unknown and into the process of learning through self-discovery.

The research journey
The research journey is important because it is the journey to self-discovery: a journey into life which I recommend for all of us who are educators. To re-search the issues above for the purposes identified required the development of a unique research design that would empower me to gain my desired out-comes. I chose longitudinal personal and collaborative experiential action research and inquiry processes, including developing autobiographical awareness (Torbert and Fisher, 1992), first, second and third person action research and inquiry (Reason, 2001), the action turn (Reason and Torbert, 2001), academically-based community service (Harkavy, 1997) and appreciative inquiry (Cooperider and Whitney, 1999). Over time I meshed together elements of these different approaches to create my own unique research design to facilitate understanding of the issues being explored. The longitudinal aspect of the research evolved into my living human inquiry as a way of life. The approach allowed me to take hook's (hook and West, 1991) advice of moving beyond the emotionally felt nature of the experience to theorise it. These research approaches brought my autobiography into contact with the lifetime journey of Diasporic Africans enabling me to develop 'autobiographical awareness' defined as 'simultaneous appreciation for lifetime and present moment for self and other' (Torbert and Fisher, 1992).

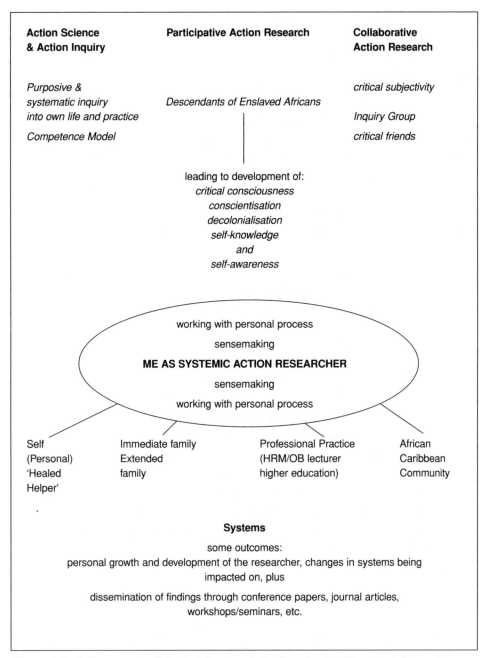

Figure 1.2: A Community Oriented Approach for Developing Bicultural Competence

Figure 1.2 is a diagrammatic representation of the research process that emerged as I inquired systematically to achieve my identified purposes. The model positions me at the centre of the total research process engaged in active sense-making as I work with the black experience, enabling me to begin to read the world critically and through *praxis* taking informed action.

Drawing on Weick's (1995) definition of 'sense-making', my active sense-making began with the realisation – the shock – of the dark side of equal opportunity codes of practice and how they are misused. In my case it was the realisation that I had not been employed on merit as I had thought but as a token to satisfy political needs and in defiance of major objections by colleagues-to-be. Over a period of years with persistent and studied sense-making I was to become clearer about my experiences. However, as Weick (1995) himself notes:

> Sense-making is tested to the extreme when people encounter an event whose occurrence is so implausible that they hesitate to report it for fear they will not be believed. In essence, these people think to themselves, it can't be, therefore it isn't.

Race is just such an experience in UK society especially in elite institutions where the phenomenon is denied even as it is being enacted. Another factor was the recognition that my sense-making as a black woman is more than likely to be disbelieved, if not ridiculed, by white colleagues.

My focal position in the research is critical to the re-humanising goal that I set myself. Fordham (1996) describes such a process as 'becoming a person'. At one and the same time I am researcher, co-researcher and researched upon as well as researching into the wider social forces and systems as they impact on me and on my ability to take action in my world effectively. The model highlights the major research methods used and the important developmental outcomes I was personally seeking from using these methods, which was critical consciousness. Some of the important outcomes of researching are highlighted as I sought critical feedback from a sceptical public.

Naming the model a 'community oriented approach' was important in that I recognised that an outward directed approach was equally as important as the inward directed approach I have identified above for the problems that I was experiencing. I was also to move backwards and forwards.

Adopting a systems approach is an acknowledgement that the process of learning itself is a system that connects me with issues in my world – a system which is determined by the issues I am addressing and through which I am united with others in a dynamic 'ecology of mind' (Bateson, 1972). Positioning myself this way is also an acknowledgement of my active participation with others (ie family, students, fellow educationalists) in the critical exploration of complex and dynamic issues which relate to the relationships between us in our physical and socio-cultural environments. I have come to understand that our common purpose is to improve our condition in the world, which is complex and problematic and without ready made answers. In the absence of known worlds my aim continues to be to 'bring forth new worlds together'.

These research approaches helped me towards self-awareness and the understanding that life unfolds and that I can be a witness to my own life and all life. I came to understand that I am much more than the black body that British society and culture have locked me into and would have me believe I am. According to generational theory (Strauss and Howe, 1991) I am now at midlife with a central role of leadership whether through parenting, teaching, directing institutions or using values but with my life chances limited by my espoused race and skin colour in Britain. It seems that race is the historical legacy that life has given me as an individual and as a member of a particular group to work through if I am to achieve my human potential and not remain stunted by the invisible workings of this legacy. Consequently I am no longer able to collude with the silence surrounding race and slavery. Slavery is abnormal and blocks self-expression.

The structure of the book
The book is written for educators, teachers and parents, and is structured so that the developmental and cognitive processes I underwent during my research journey are as transparent as possible. I hope that other educators will be as challenged as I was when I realised how the blockage of race was working itself out in our lives and my responsibility as an educator not to continue to be a part of the problem. Chapter two contains vignettes culled from my life experiences between 1959 and 2004 when I turned 50. These vignettes provide important insights into the black experience in the context of the white experience across the life span, telling their own story of what life has been like as a result of my unconscious assimilation into British culture. The lack of opportunity for evaluating the black life experience is revealed and how this means that important connections between experiences are missed. Chapter three draws on the literature researching the black experience in organisational life. Connections between the two sets of experiences in chapters two and three are striking and provide a more holistic view of the black experience that precipitated a crisis of meaning for me. In chapter four I go back to Africa, the Caribbean and immigration to England in the 1950s to better understand how the black experience came about in the first place.

The politics of positionality is crystallised in terms of how enslaved Africans were recreated into blacks and positioned relative to Europeans who were re-created into whites. This background experience is important in understanding what we need to know to achieve social justice and inclusion for all children in British society.

The research in chapters two, three and four was crucial to my developing autobiographical awareness, self-knowledge and my awareness as an educator. It reveals the constructed nature of black and white experiences suggesting dysfunctional cultural legacies which we educators unconsciously transmit to future generations. It also provides important insights into the dysfunctional relationship between blacks and whites in British society which as educators we have a responsibility to work with. That 'race' has been thrown as a veil over the consciousness of both blacks and whites hiding from us the reality of what being human means, becomes apparent especially in terms of the way the institution of slavery transformed our ancestors and affects us still.

In chapter five I explore what it means to be a whole human being in order to understand how the recreation of two groups of the human family has been achieved. This analysis reveals culture as the definitive key, confirming my earlier conceptualisation of the bicultural competence matrix. Chapter six constitutes an analysis of British culture and how the division of the human family into blacks and whites is maintained today. The institution of social interaction is shown as responsible for maintaining the black-white duality and therefore social inequality beyond our conscious awareness. The analysis presents both blacks and whites, the active and passive maintainers and perpetuators of social inequality, with important challenges.

In chapter seven I engage with the consequences of the previous chapters for my inner world to improve my own practical knowing. This chapter brought me face to face with the reasons for the psychic disorientation, confusion and despair that had dogged my life to that point. I was also able to witness the dysfunctional legacies I was unconsciously transmitting as both a parent and a teacher and how the process worked.

The findings of the research to this point confirm the salience of the bicultural competence thesis and its applicability to all members of British society because of the central place held by race and black and white cultures. This is discussed in depth in chapter eight where the bicultural competence matrix and the five dimensional human being models are recommended as human development tools which can be used to underpin our educational practice. The imperative of conscious bicultural competence is discussed in chapter nine, where the significance of educators, teachers and parents, as cultural workers, developing conscious bicultural competence, is explored. The implications of the previous chapters for the DoEAs are discussed in chapter ten and ideas are offered as to how we can work with our lives as a group with the aim of transforming it. The final chapter draws out the major themes identified as being centred round the issues of knowledge, history, culture, power and identity, and reflects on the major themes that have emerged.

A note on terminology

A primary finding of my research is that 'black' and 'white' as terms to refer to the descendants of enslaved Africans (DoEAs) and to the descendants of slave-owners (DoSOs) respectively are dehumanising. As a result I tend to use these latter terms throughout, reflecting my own re-humanising agenda. However, the term black is widely used in the literature to refer to the DoEAs: I have retained it when needed for common understanding and in order not to confuse the issue. The Office of the National Statistician (ONS, 2003) also acknowledges a defining feature of the ethnic majority in Britain as being 'white', thus confirming the accepted usage of these two identifiers. Writing of DoEAs and DoSOs is an attempt to move beyond black and white and to position our relationship relative to the other historically. References to blacks and whites refer mainly to those DoEAs and DoSOs who continue to be locked into unconsciousness within the boundaries of the black-white duality where they cannot conceive themselves other than as 'black' or 'white'.

Another problematic term is that of 'race'. In my enlightened understanding there exists only one human race: *homo sapiens*. Where I use the term, sparingly, it should be understood as a social construction developed to put in place the power differential between the DoEAs and the DoSOs which many have accepted as a reality.

Culture is another concept requiring brief discussion. My main use of the term draws on Noble's (1985) definition of culture being a design for living – culture as process, as fluid and moving. References to black and white cultures therefore refer to two different designs for living based on the power differential put in place between blacks and whites during slavery: for whites, a superior design for living and, for blacks, an inferior design for living. Black culture, as distinct from African culture, is seen to be the child of the British empire, as in the design for living imposed on enslaved Africans by white slave owners. Enslaved Africans mediated this victim culture imposed by whites with elements of African culture as well as elements of British and European culture as they imitated the design for living of their white masters.

Ionescu's (Alchin, 2003) reminder that we are all human beings has particular relevance to those living within the bounds of black culture: in penetrating the veneer of black culture I have been able to locate a British African-Caribbean culture struggling to give birth to itself.

2

Psychic disorientation, confusion and despair (1)

Anything you attack will fight back. Chances are if you have a problem, it is bigger than you; it crept up on you or you didn't know what you were doing in the first place. Don't attack your problems. Face them, confess them, understand what they are – that is the process. The process teaches and brings a richness that will help you avoid future problems ... the process keeps you in the moment and you must be in the moment to fully experience the solution.
(Vanzant (1993): June 22).

Identity achieved by victimisation is pathology ... identity formation and human development, generally, is an essentially transactive process composed simultaneously of individual striving and social support.
(Hoover *et al*, 1997)

Can a man create life, then abandon his creation because its appearance horrifies him? To whom are its actions then attributable: the creature or the being who brought about its existence?
(Berardinelli, 1994) referring to Frankenstein's Monster

Too much has happened to put right. I would need another life. No, several lives. Another hundred years. No, more, to unravel this knotted mess. Too tired even to begin. Wouldn't know where or how. Maybe what's done is done. It cannot now be undone, only understood. Others might understand. They will look and see a man who has too many days and nights. They will see a time when a short life was the best life to live under such conditions. The master is daylight, the slave is night. A complete day needs both light and dark. The day cannot be broken in two to leave each half to itself. Nor can the master hope to rule the day and the night along with it forever. Slavery is a long day of the master over the slave and of nights turned to days. But how long can the master's daylight continue to rule our nights?
(D'Aguiar, 1995:136-137)

Introduction

The decision to research my own life was the first transformative step I took. I was for the first time acknowledging my life as being worthy of study and began to use the type of self-reflection that the race taboo inhibits. Surfacing and sharing the vignettes that follow is a deliberate violation of the race taboo. It allowed important connections between the experiences that had led me into an existential crisis of meaning in the first place. The vignettes cover most of the 50 years since the famous Windrush arrived in England with 417 passengers from Britain's colonies. They give a vivid picture of why I found myself in an existential crisis of meaning as I gradually internalised the experience of being a member of a group with a stigmatised collective identity and a predetermined place in British society. The vignettes raise questions about the taken-for-granted assumptions we carry but rarely test out for their truth.

As I have researched to bring to the surface what it means to be black in Britain, I find similarities between my experience and the Monster in Mary Shelley's *Frankenstein*. In Frankenstein the Monster tells his story within the larger novel, providing insights into his process of learning about his surroundings, language and emotions to reveal the psychology of human development. His narrative substantiates the internal conflicts and misperceptions he uses in defence of his actions. Using autobiographical research as the main source for developing awareness of the consequences of the recreation of enslaved Africans by the white British into something other than a whole human being feels rather like this. This is especially as I experience white silence as an important means of preventing me from waking up from enforced unconsciousness so that our silenced story as DoEAs can be surfaced and added to the wider narrative of the human story.

Background

I arrived in England from Jamaica, the plantation society *par excellence* during the period of slavery, in autumn 1959. My father came in 1954, the year of my birth, to work as a labourer doing the menial work whites did not want to do in the post-war boom. My mother arrived in 1958 and my sister and I joined our parents the following year. By then my father had purchased a home for us. My parents were to have four more children. My mother's main role in life has been a homemaker, having never worked outside the home. Both my parents come from rural parts of Jamaica where they received only limited formal education. Our social life as a family centred round the activities of the Baptist church, its Christian philosophy underpinning our lives.

The social context (1959-1969) Headlines proclaimed news of: 'race' riots flaring in Notting Hill Gate after white youths taunted black immigrants with racist slogans, which precipitated racial tension throughout the period; demands for tightening immigration controls; creation of the race relations board; Enoch Powell foreseeing 'rivers of blood'; 'race' as a prevalent issue in US reported across the world: Malcolm X and Martin Luther King gunned down.

Age 5 (1959)
Entering the British school system at the age of 5, I made the unconscious decision to be like the white children because of the negative way I saw the white teachers relating to black children. I unconsciously decided not to be myself because I could see that to be black was not a good thing in the eyes of my white teachers. Over time I became Mr Petts' pet!

Age 8 (1962)
I am shooed from the front door of my best friend's home when her mother sees a black child on her doorstep. My best friend is white.

Age 11 (1965)
Asked to show the class how to cook rice as this is the staple diet of blacks and I am black.

Receive repeated requests for inside information on the 'black problem' from my white teachers and classmates.

Correcting someone in class who used the word 'vex', telling them the correct word was 'bex' as my parents said, and being laughed at.

Age 12 (1966)
Standing at the front of the dinner queue with my best friends (all white) I am rushed by a group of black girls who had decided they were going to be first into dinner without queuing. Jean looked at them in disgust and said 'Look at those ignorant black bastards' – only afterwards remembering that I was black, perhaps when she saw the look on my face. Jean said: 'Not you Gloria, you're different'.

Age 13 (1967)
Having been in a top academic group since the first year – one of only two black girls the other being from Ghana – I find myself singled out and identi-fied as not good enough to do O-levels when GCE choices were being made. Instead I was told that CSEs would be better for me. I challenged this decision by repeatedly bringing my mother to the school to support me in my deter-mination to do GCEs.

Age 15 (1969)

I let out some of my feelings by querying something a white classmate did and was harshly reprimanded by the teacher: 'we don't expect that from you!'

Social Context (1970-1979): Police and blacks clash in Notting Hill. Police accused of being racially prejudiced. Enoch Powell predicts an 'explosion' unless there is a massive repatriation scheme for immigrants. Immigration Bill ends right of commonwealth citizens to settle in Britain. Muggings, violence and looting mar the annual Notting Hill Carnival; Thatcher makes statement about England being 'swamped'.

Age 18 (1972)

At 18 observing the shock on the head-teacher's face at my exit interview on realising I had gained 7 O-levels and 2 A-levels during my school career. My teachers had had low expectations for me as a black child. No one had realised that I had managed this level of academic achievement. I had been totally unsupported throughout my school career and had spent much of my time struggling to deny the stereotypes I was expected to satisfy to prove myself black and therefore inferior.

Age 19 (1973)

Being asked by a black barber in Brixton, when he heard that I had been accepted on a Personnel Management course of study, whether I really expected whites to give me a job in their personnel department where they kept staff records.

Age 20 (1974)

Being unable to gain a job after college commensurate with my qualifications and the type of jobs my white peers got. Finding myself invited for interviews for each job based on my CV and eventually realising that it was because I had classified myself as British on my application form I had gained an interview. This insight was confirmed when invitations to interviews stopped immediately I give my nationality as Jamaican. The word of one white man has remained in my mind over the years: 'you have a formidable school record for a black girl, haven't you?'

Police raiding the black youth club held at The Swan in Stockwell on a Sunday evening and hitting young people indiscriminately with their batons as they picked out black males to be taken to the station in the back of their police vans. Breathing a sigh of relief that I was not male as I headed home alone, having lost my girlfriend in the frenzy and fright of the incident.

Age 21 (1975)

When taking out life insurance, filling in my occupation on the form as a 'clerical officer' and being told: 'surely you mean clerical assistant?'

Excuses consistently found by senior staff to ensure that I – as the sole black member of staff – am sent out of the staff meetings (to make tea) when issues they do not want to discuss in my presence come up on the agenda.

Age 22 (1976)

Began voluntary service with Brixton Community Law Centre to support black youth during the time of the 'Sus' law and witnessing black youth systematically and unfairly targeted by the police.

Age 23 (1977)

Accepted job as Assistant Community Relations Officer with Newham Community Relations Council where I was responsible for working with 'alienated black youth'. Left the job within a year because of controversy and confusion that surrounds the issue.

Age 25 (1979)

Reprimanded by a white male colleague whose wife complained I had not spoken to her courteously enough when she phoned the office.

Social context (1980-1989) – Race riots in Brixton. Publication of the Nationality Bill which would replace current citizenship with three new categories. Seventeen people hurt and 23 arrested during a protest at police handling of the Deptford fire. At least 80 people including 40 police injured when 300 skinheads and 400 Asians clash in Southall. Brixton is ablaze as black youths riot; Thatcher condemns the Brixton riots as 'utterly wrong ... unjustified ... criminal'.

Age 29 (1983)

Return to education after the birth of my first child to gain vocational skills so I can become self-employed – a result of my disillusionment about the experience of being black in Britain.

Aged 30 (1984)

Coming top of the class as a mature returner to education and being told by the lecturer: 'it's not true then what they say is it?' 'What do they say?' I ask. 'That all blacks are stupid.'

Being cornered in the changing rooms by white students demanding to know how I had managed to cheat my way through the exams, so shocked were they that I was top of the class.

Age 33 (1987)

Returning from holiday abroad having used my Jamaican passport – a conscious decision to be a first class citizen of Jamaica as opposed to a second class citizen of Britain – and being given three months to verify my right to stay in the country. Failure to do so would mean deportation. The rudeness and disrespect I endured as a black person from the immigration officers at both the airport and Lunar House is still crystal clear in my memory.

Age 34 (1988)

Told by my new employer that I was their star turn since being both black and a woman I satisfied current equal opportunity requirements.

When I asked why I was being paid less than white colleagues my employer told me that the only way he had been able to get white colleagues to agree to my joining the staff was to start me on a lower salary than much younger white counterparts recruited at the same time.

Noticing that despite being said to be lacking in experience and qualifications I was placed in classrooms to teach the more challenging part-time students while my much younger white peers with espoused experience and qualifications – as witnessed in reward packages – were apprenticed to more senior staff to induct them into the classroom environment.

I am told by my employer that I need to gained additional qualifications if I am to gain the parity with white colleagues I desire.

Age 35 (1989)

Told by my line manager that I am not employed as an academic to think, but to do as I am told!

Told by teachers, at his private school, that my eldest son's behaviour is 'disruptive and aggressive' and that he is 'a distracting influence' in the classroom. I suggested that since he was fourth in a class of sixteen children that he might be bored. Within weeks he was down to 16th position in a class of sixteen children. His report noted that his reading ability was poor. How could this statement be written about a child who regularly delivered scripture readings to a large church congregation? Tests at a private assessment centre showed the assessment carried out by the school to be incorrect, as I knew it had been. Was my son being penalised because I had dared to question the school's version of events?

Social context (1990-1999)

Stephen Lawrence's racist murder in 1993; The Lawrence's private prosecution case against their son's suspected murders; Jury returns verdict of unlawful killing in a completely unprovoked racist attack by five white males; complaint made to the Police Complaints Association (PCA) about the nature of the inquiry; Macpherson report identifies police as riddled with pernicious and institutionalised racism.

Age 36 (1990)
Warned by a white colleague who had seen a black student in my office that being seen with black students could be perceived as colluding with them!

Writing my identity down as 'African-Caribbean' in an article and a white colleague changing it to 'Afro-Caribbean'!

Age 37 (1991)
I am told by a senior white male colleague that even I must be surprised at my own achievements since everyone knows blacks are born mentally inferior to whites.

Asked by my son how would I respond if I were accused of being a disgrace to the black race?

Age 38 (1992)
Having gained the required qualifications – post-graduate diploma in management studies – I am told by management that I need a still higher level of qualification – a master's degree – to gain parity with white colleagues. None of my white colleagues has a master's degree.

Sent to 'Coventry' by white colleagues because I asked questions about being treated differently because of being black in opposition to what our equal opportunities policy stated.

Told by the new class teacher that 'there is nothing special about him' referring to my 7 year-old son and witnessing him becoming progressively demotivated. Offering to do a classroom session with the children enabled me to see that my son had been placed on the 'special' table with other black boys who were perceived to be problems.

Age 39 (1993)
I overhear a white male colleague refer to me as 'uppity nigger'.

After a verbal racial attack directed at us by a white woman in the doctor's surgery, I turn to my son and ask: why us? My son responds: it's because we are 75 percent white and only 25 percent black!

Age 40 (1994)
Noting that not even the MBA I gained – with distinction – was good enough. Told I now needed management experience to qualify for the parity of treat-

ment with white colleagues I was *still* seeking. I gradually came to the realisation that qualifications in my case were being used as an obstacle course and the assumption was that as a black person I was mentally inferior so unlikely to gain the required qualification.

Laughed at by white colleagues on seeing the publicity brochure on which I had been positioned as an afterthought at the bottom of the page. In addition, I am labelled as the 'ethnic expert' as the sole black member of staff in the school. None of the qualifications I had been told I needed to gain were acknowledged on the brochure, unlike those of my white colleagues, one of whom had been attributed qualifications she did not have.

Aged 41 (1995)
Internal grievance raised which ended up in industrial (now employment) tribunal proceedings.

Told that if I persist in raising race as an issue I'll make things worse for other blacks.

Aged 42 (1996)
A Ghanaian colleague decides to return home to Ghana because he cannot cope with the experience of being black in Britain. He says: 'blacks in Britain must develop alligator skins to survive here.'

Age 43 (1997)
Gained PhD from University of Bath – *Towards Bicultural Competence: Researching for Personal and Professional Transformations*. I had gained academic and intellectual knowledge about the black experience but couldn't apply my knowledge in daily life because of the force of the race taboo, the fear around the subject and my own internalised silences underpinned by white silence.

Age 44 (1998)
I develop various psychosomatic illnesses due to the stress of my inferiorisation, marginality, lack of value, sense of expendability, fear, shame, lack of collegiate support, and general sense of isolation based on being black. Made worse by feeling that the knowledge I had gained could not be used in the university because of the fear of race that permeated my institutional experience. This made me fearful, even of myself.

Since the initial demand in 1987 that I needed more qualifications to gain parity with my white peers, I had gained a post-graduate diploma in management studies, a MBA with distinction; a post-graduate certificate in Multi-Ethnic Psychodynamic Counselling and a PhD – but still had not gained the parity I had been promised and desired.

Felt ashamed of my inability to be a positive role model for my children despite all my efforts. The clear message being transmitted to my children and students was that gaining academic qualifications is not worthwhile if it is to gain equality of opportunity in Britain as a black person.

Social context (2000 onwards): Race Relations Amendment Act 2000; Introduction of citizenship education in school system; Bernard Coard's 'How the West Indian Child is made Educationally Subnormal in the British school system' reprinted with contemporary chapters showing how little has changed; crisis of black boys underachievement in London schools.

Age 46 (2000)
After long absences from work because of ill health I made the inner decision to begin to work with issues as they arose – which I had self-protectively still been shying away from. This meant I would now have to engage with the fear, shame, silence, ambivalence and denial surrounding the black experience as I was living it.

Taking over supervision of a black middle-aged man on a master's programme who had chosen to explore institutionalised racism in the police force, where he was employed, I learn that he has been warned by a white male professor that he is not allowed to touch the subject with a barge-pole. Is this because I am to be his supervisor? This student perceives me, as a black member of staff, to be powerless to help him get his degree, so chooses the safe topic of job design instead.

Age 47 (2001)
Short-listed for national award. This suggests I am 'good enough' for something after all. Challenged myself to apply for Principal Lecturer during annual promotion rounds while noting how strongly I had been socialised not to aspire for these positions. Application turned down: the feedback was that I needed management experience and more publications.

Asked by a white female colleague: 'who gave *you* a remit for change?'

White male professor writes letter to head of division and other senior white colleagues threatening to undermine me with learners on the unit I am leading if he is forced to co-teach on the team working with me. I am not sent a copy of this letter.

Age 48 (2002)
I gained national award and research fellowship for demonstrating excellence in teaching and learning. The view is shared that I am a token black award-holder.

I make the decision to use Academically-Based Community Service research approach and to place a strategic focus on the British African Caribbean community. My organisational experiences alongside research have finally pushed me to realise that this is the group to which I belong to and where, therefore, my energies should focus.

Despite overt request for management support, including using the appraisal process, none forthcoming. Continue to witness how my open and deliberate requests for management support around the black experience is consistently ignored by management. The experience of being marginalised, inferiorised, made invisible and undervalued increases with my frustration.

Realised I am still being used as a token black, despite constant official denial, to satisfy equal opportunity requirements and that I have no other value to the institution beyond that status.

Issues related to treatment as a black member of staff raised with employers ignored. Ends up in second employment tribunal hearing as I pushed for an official response to the issues raised as a means of breaking the silence I had internalised and which was being re-imposed and re-confirmed by the institution's response to me.

Age 49 (2003)
Acknowledging white refusal to accept or even entertain my interpretation of reality as a black woman. A white perspective dictates that none of my experiences have anything to do with my being a black woman: I have got it wrong, don't understand and have a chip on my shoulder.

Deciding to home educate my youngest son at the point of transfer to secondary school given my enlightened understanding of our experience as black people in Britain.

Hearing statements such as 'it is because of the subject she teaches why she knows so much'; 'she is an aware black' and the question 'how come you are so articulate on the subject of race?' confirmed my growing understanding that white culture does not foster the unconsciousness that typifies black culture.

Age 50 (2004)
Acting on what I implicitly and explicitly understand is necessary for human flourishing I am able to see more clearly how British culture is structured, implemented and perpetuated to maintain the *status quo* by maintaining power differentials between blacks and whites.

Analysis of the vignettes

The implications of these vignettes for us as parents and teachers of white and black children become immediately apparent. As a parent and an educator I knew that I could not allow this non-generative cultural heritage to continue to be transmitted. The first theme that jumps out from these vignettes is the predetermined nature of what it means to be black in British society: unentitled, inferior to whites, afforded low teacher and other expectations and an outsider. The second is how clearly the vignettes reveal that it is whites who determine what it means to be black. The third theme is not overtly visible but has been an over-riding feature of my life experience and the reason I am sharing these vignettes in the presence of whites: fear. Fear of acknowledging what it means for me to be black in the white presence and imagination. Fear of acknowledging the real. Fear of naming the private reality behind the public image. These experiences are hidden behind a wall of silence, causing me to doubt my own ability to know what I know. And so we see that black socialisation and culture as administered by whites works to inhibit growth and results in a stunted personality.

My crisis was caused by coming face to face with the societal limits placed on me as a black person and beyond which I was unable to move however hard I tried. What does it mean to be predetermined? It means being locked into a role and a way of being from which it seems impossible to escape. This conjures Whitechapel's anguish (D'Anguiar, 1994): 'Too much has happened to put right. I would need another life. No, several lives. Another hundred years. No, more, to unravel this knotted mess. Too tired even to begin ...'

It is notable that there is no evidence in the vignettes of a strong family or community infrastructure supporting me in my journey through life. Instead I am seen from childhood to be making survival choices on my own, without any real adult guidance. Black children it seems are cast into the world as orphans to struggle on their own given the helplessness of their parents where understanding of British culture is concerned. My mother enters the vignettes on two occasions when I brought her to school to put pressure on teachers to let me sit GCEs and later when I make reference to the differences in use of the English language at school and at home. I recognise in this second instance how I lost confidence in my parents' ability to equip me with appropriate English usage to be successful in school and society. My most influential socialisation is seen to come from the school system, with no culture of origin being taught in the home. This omission on the part of my parents confirms my inculturation into British culture beyond my conscious awareness.

The other two primary socialisation institutions, family and church, encouraged me towards wholesale assimilation, preferring me to associate with the 'good' whites rather than 'bad' blacks. The lessons learned from school are seen to be marginalisation, inferiorisation, 'not being good enough', lack of favourable teacher expectations – and my learning to appease teachers in order to gain their patronage so I could succeed as a black child. Whenever I do act against the socialised predetermined grain I am forcefully put back in my predetermined place. The vignettes reveal that whether I decide to be silent and collude or to name the marginalisation, inferiorisation and discrimination I am experiencing: the outcome is the same – no progress – but the costs of 'knowing' cost me dear.

My lack of a confrontational presence is apparent throughout the excerpts. Generally I use non-challenging, conflict avoidance behaviours as a survival strategy. The vignettes portray me as a watcher or witness of the environment and how it impacts on me as a black person. I am seen to make mainly inner choices about how to respond so that I can survive. It seems that as I witnessed white behaviours I became increasingly silent, growing more fearful of what lay behind the silences, which I tacitly know is not good. The desire to gain parity with whites through self-improvement is a strong theme throughout. This is probably because of my ahistorical and apolitical socialisation as well as my belief in a meritocracy, despite evidence to the contrary. Overall the vignettes suggest that I had woven together my own survival strategy which I eventually exhausted because of its focus on pleasing the ethnic majority.

Up until my MBA research in 1992 I lived in survival mode, locked into a state of unconsciousness. It was my MBA research that unearthed silence as the most significant theme underpinning my life experience: it was internalised and was externally imposed on me. Thus I began the journey from unconsciousness to consciousness. Surfacing the tacit and taboo knowledge which was illustrative of issues to be faced on the unconscious bicultural competence quadrant where I positioned myself threw me into a deeper crisis of despondency. Life threatening illnesses in the latter part of the nineties and the breakdown of my marriage undermined my ability to engage practically with the issues that had surfaced. In the throes of ill-health I realised that my health problems were a direct result of my failure to honour myself and the messages my body was sending me. My decision in 2001 to engage with issues as they arose, as opposed to continuing in denial, avoidance, fear and repression was a decision for life and health instead of existing as the living dead. This was the period of my most significant learning as I began to challenge my assumptions using the principles of the Action Turn (Reason and Torbert, 2001). This meant moving beyond my fears and taking informed action. I experienced the real limitations of being black in British society as societal forces sought to re-impose the silence I was intent on breaking. My life since 2001 has been about taking up the challenge of learning to live as a whole human being, an interesting experience when the norm of society is unconsciousness and dehumanisation.

3

Psychic disorientation, confusion and despair (2)

Introduction

My consciousness had been shaped by the experiences described in previous chapters in ways of which I had been largely unaware until I started autobiographical research. Researching the literature allowed me to gain wider insights into my lived experiences which are not a part of the education process that DoEAs undergo in Britain. Reviewing the literature was also important as I intended to use this knowledge to develop my conscious bicultural competence to enable me to support DoEA learners in the education system. The deafening silence around race acknowledged by Matsuura in 2004 is the defining theme of the management literature in terms of the British experience. Much of the literature used here is drawn from the African-American experience, providing important insights into how the race taboo plays itself out in practice in the British context. This chapter provides important insights into the organisational and longer-term issues that DoEAs face if they are able to break out of the culture of poverty and deprivation which underpins the black experience. Black parents struggling with the issues detailed in the world of work will recognise the double bind in which they are caught up and why they have a limited ability to support their children more effectively.

Black disadvantage

While developing autobiographical awareness was guiding me towards dropping the negative black identity as a means of self-identification, surveying the literature makes it clear that DoEAs have taken on the black identifier as it has been conferred on us. In African-American literature the term is used synonymously with African-American by both blacks and whites. In this chapter I continue to use the term black to refer to DoEAs in keeping with the literature. The literature shows that the disadvantage experienced by black people in the workplace has been well documented in the US but not in the UK. In the US black people (DoEAs) are one of numerous ethnic minority groups and are known as African-Americans. In Britain, England is perceived as belonging to the English, who are currently struggling with the fall-out of empire in terms of the diversity of peoples and cultures now present on their shores. As a result, minority issues are not high on the agenda unless they are forced there, as they are being pushed by the Muslims. Copying the black American example, black people in Britain have increasingly been referred to as African-Caribbeans. More rare, however, is the acknowledgment of our British heritage as seen in the identifier British African-Caribbean. This can be understood as either denial or as lack of acknowledgement of the unique experience of this group, as well as an outcome of the race taboo and complicity with our oppression. Cashmore's (1989) view is that the government uses a policy of containment to manage the issue in Britain. The silence in the literature about the experience of black people reflected the silence I had surfaced in my inner world in my MBA research (Bravette, 1993).

What research there is shows substantial evidence of racial discrimination against black people in the workplace and labour market in Britain. Studies suggest that it is the acceptability of the black person in terms of white standards such as attitudes and appearance that decide on their fate. This was something I learned early in school. McKellar (1989) confirms this when she highlights the necessity to be bicultural in the field of education and in the workplace and to prioritise developing a British cultural perspective during college and at work if career progression is the aim. Black people must take on the cultural capital of the dominant society if they want to be successful in society by silencing their own lived experiences in order to be accepted. Managers who are black must manage their work and how others respond to them, particularly when racist statements and behaviours whether overt, covert, intended and unintended are directed towards them. They need to develop conflict resolution skills in view of the experiences they are likely to encounter.

The literature clearly shows that the burden of being black is overtly placed on the victim of this social construction to manage. Significant involvement of blacks in organisations is often restricted by stereotypes which hinder access and treatment. When the black person is the only one in their workgroup and when black recruits are viewed by white organisational members as incompetent simply because equal opportunities is involved in their selection

(Pettigrew and Martin, 1987) these problems arise. Research findings suggest that race has a negative effect on the career aspirations and opportunities of black people in organisations and, importantly, that it is a normalised experience. This normalisation supports the black complicity I had witnessed in my own life. Carter (1994) describes modern forms of racial prejudice as subtler and ostensibly non-racial, and which is minimised by politicians, the courts and political parties who claim that race is no longer a significant factor. This can be likened to neo-racism described as the more sophisticated, subtle and indirect forms of racism that are evidenced by individual white attitudes and behaviours: 'Today, neo-racism is the danger in the integrated community and its assault is most commonly aimed at undermining the black's self-confidence and self-worth.' (Dickens and Dickens, 1991)

On the experiences of African-Americans Dickens and Dickens (1991) make the following very important statement:

> Some ... black professionals became successful, but at a great cost to their self-esteem, self-respect and self-concept. These blacks paid a price that must no longer be extracted from them ... Much black talent has been lost as a result of both racism and sexism.

Their statement resonates strongly with my own experience of being black in the UK. It was the cost to my self-esteem, self-respect and self-concept that eventually pushed me into a crisis of meaning. I became determined to understand the issues and to identify the salient features and characteristics of what it means to be black in UK society so that I could transform it in my own life-world.

Organisational experiences
Dickens and Dickens (1991) provide a framework for black aspiring and current managers to help them understand and plan for their experiences in organisations. One key characteristic they focus on is the criterion of success that a black person uses to assess their achievement in their organisational life. Dickens and Dickens express the questionable view that too many black people have the unrealistic criterion of equality with their white counterparts which suggests that my aspirations for equality with white colleagues were unrealistic. They identify four phases – Entry, Adjusting, Planned Growth and Success – the black manager needs to be cognisant of. The features of each phase, including possible emotional reactions, job skill levels, and behaviours are also shared. Their analysis of the perceptions of blacks at the Entry phase into organisations is of particular interest: blacks are 'grateful', 'feel fortunate', 'are not wanting to make waves' and 'are seeking acceptance'.

These are behaviours I recognised and which it became evident I am as a black person in the academy expected to show given the numbers of time I have been told I am lucky to have a job as a lecturer in higher education. Dickens and Dickens observe that blacks are often beset by confusion and self-doubt. They say that although not all blacks believe all the negative stereotypes and perceptions society holds about them and their competence, they usually internalise these negative perceptions to some degree. Also that many blacks hope that the organisation will disregard their blackness and judge them as their white colleagues are judged: on their merits. The primary behaviours identified in this phase are 'fit-in' and 'avoidance' and are in-dicative of the individual's need to either overcome their blackness to belong or to avoid the unpleasant task of any interaction with whites beyond getting the job done.

According to Dickens and Dickens (1991), while blacks have the technical competence when they join an organisation they will not be given the oppor-tunity to develop management skills and are seldom part of the informal net-working system of the organisation. Stanton-Salazar (1997) points to the role of underlying exclusionary forces located in and across institutional domains. He identifies social antagonisms and divisions which exist in wider society which operate to problematise, if not undermine, black access to oppor-tunities and resources that are taken for granted by whites – as seen in neo-pigmentocracies below. This effectively limits the 'social distribution of pos-sibilities' for blacks. This was the experience the vignettes from my life reveal which encouraged me to employ action research as a means of developing important group specific skills outside the workplace to enhance my possi-bilities in the institution.

Several important points made by Dickens and Dickens warrant analysis in this study. The first is their statement that 'A black manager's survival depends on their ability to have sound bicultural skills'. I equate this with my own con-cept of conscious bicultural competence shown in the top right quadrant of the matrix. The third phase of planned growth they identify as a period of consciously structured activity for black managers. They say: 'Since the organisation may not become less racist, black managers begin to accept the responsibility for changing their own style and methods of operating'. I opted to do precisely that through the use of personal and collaborative action re-search and inquiry along with developing autobiographical awareness-in-action (bottom right quadrant of the matrix). They suggest that in the success phase black managers at all times need to maintain awareness of their black-ness and how this impacts on the organisation. Interestingly, they note that making mistakes or failing is not an option for black managers! However, they do make the telling statement: 'To forget the impact of racism is tantamount to losing or giving up one's survival instinct'. The ultimate goal is job mastery, which places the individual's capability, competence, action and other leadership issues in his or her own hands and not in those of the organisation. So, blacks are expected to demonstrate profound meta-cognitive skills and capabilities – yet they are espoused to be inferior. If they cannot demonstrate such skills they have to dumb down to survive or they have to leave the organisation sooner or later.

Inter-group theory

The position taken by Dickens and Dickens (1991) resonates with Proudford's (1999) work on the stigmatisation of differences and in which she cites Alderfer and Smith's (1982) inter-group perspective. Proudford focuses on patterns of relationship between groups in the institutional context. The inter-group perspective aids this discussion by acknowledging that the dynamics taking place between groups are generally not discussable within the organisational context especially where the colour-blind, 'no problem here' approach prevails. Alderfer and Smith argue that individuals and groups are continuously engaged in a process of managing the tensions that arise from being members of different identity (race, ethnicity and gender) and organisation (task, function, hierarchy) groups. They also argue that the pattern of identity and organisation groups in a particular context, which is termed embeddedness, influences behaviour and they distinguish between congruent embeddedness and incongruent embeddedness. Congruent embeddedness powers relationships among groups at the organisational level and reflects power relations at the societal level. In terms of race, most organisations and specifically higher education institutions display congruent embeddedness: the white majority that hold positions of power especially at the upper echelons of the institution. Incongruent embeddedness occurs when blacks hold high status positions at the organisational level as opposed to power relationships at the societal levels.

Perceptual salience arises from the relationship between the group memberships engaged in the interaction and the composition of the organisational context and reflects the extent to which individuals are congruently or incongruently embedded in the organisation. White women tend towards gender salience whereas for black women either race or gender might be salient. In the UK the perceptual salience of the white majority frames inter-group preference and determine what issues can be discussed in the institutional context because of its congruent embeddedness. That the white majority adopt a 'no problem here' stance, compounded by a colour-blind approach, is taken for granted. This is normalised within organisational life in cross-racial inter-actions.

Leicester and Lovell (1994) point out how institutional agents in the UK are willing to respond to questions on disability and gender but become silent on issues of race. This results in a silencing process that invariably limits the ability of blacks – marginal members of the institution – to engage in any form of productive dialogue or to develop their ability to interact with whites about race related issues. Institutional agents who adopt a colour-blind approach in adherence to the race taboo effectively keep race off the institutional agenda as a topic which cannot be discussed (Arygris and Schon, 1996). Lukes (1974) describes this as the covert and silent use of power. In this context black pro-fessionals like Dickens and Dickens and other academic researchers have become normalised to the *status quo*, placing the onus on individual black employees/professionals to manage their blackness more effectively.

The use of inter-group theory points us to what could become possible in our organisations if we were to use it as a means of managing difference. Alderfer (1998) suggests that an alternative and sincere theory of groups for a multi-cultural society has different underpinning assumptions. For example:

- The theory would not think in terms of individual versus the group but rather frame the relationships as about individuals and groups

- Groups would be taken as whole entities in their own right, that is, as significantly different from the sum of their individual members

- The theory would acknowledge that, regardless of role, individuals do not leave behind their identity-group affiliations – namely, that we all are influenced as individuals intra-psychically and as group repre-sentatives by our several group memberships, including race, ethni-city, gender, generation, and family

- The theory would indicate that we are less objective in the traditional sense when we ignore or deny these effects than when we accept and embrace them

- The theory would base knowledge of group and inter-group relations in part on taking account of unconscious processes in individuals, in groups, and between groups

People whose actions are influenced by these theoretical assumptions be-have differently from those who hold the established rational view of groups as traditionally presented in the business schools and in practice. Alderfer (1998) maintains that traditional theories of groups not developed for diverse

34

workgroups are out of date because they both consciously and unconsciously keep 'us' and 'our group' (the white congruently embedded) too much at the centre of how whites think about human beings in the world. Alderfer also acknowledges that holders of theories about groups, whether explicit or tacit, generally do not think of themselves as being explained by the theories they hold. They thus tacitly place themselves as outside the laws of human behaviour. Inter-group theory explains why my attempts to acknowledge myself as the DoEA and the concerns I have as a member of this group in the institutional context are repeatedly ignored by management.

Neopigmentocracies

In their discussion of career dynamics Thomas and Alderfer (1989) offer an interesting analysis of the experience of blacks in organisations. Their analysis confirms many of the insights provided by Dickens and Dickens, Stanton-Salazar and Proudford. Thomas and Alderfer cite Wells and Jennings (1983) who posit the view that organisations do not function as meritocracies where black people are concerned. Instead they function as 'neopigmentocracies', which they define as follows:

> The neopigmentocracy is characterised by the existence of laws stating the enfranchisement of all individuals irrespective of race accompanied, however, by a psychological mindset on the part of the dominant race that reinforces a sense of entitlement characteristic of a racially caste society in South Africa (Vickery, 1974). In the neopigmentocracy, access to resources is unlimited for whites as a group while restricted for blacks, with only a few blacks being allowed to reach significant positions of authority and control over economic resources. Blacks may attain 'threshold' or acceptable positions but as a group are excluded from the management hegemony. In these organisations, persons are systemically excluded from the general mobility process be it contest, sponsored or tournament, especially as they move further up the corporate ladder.

This passage resonates with my experience in Britain, especially in relation to the gap between what is claimed and what is actually done in practice where race is an issue. The existence of laws stating equality whilst a psychological mindset of white entitlement is enacted is what Ani (1994) describes as the 'rhetorical ethic' which is defined as, culturally structured hypocrisy designed to disarm the racial other. This outcome falls within the murky realms of institutionalised racism (Macpherson, 1999). Overall the literature is clear that the black skin colour places a big burden on black people – the black 'penalty' that is normalised in Britain and America. The insights into these unfolding dynamics which are revealed through the literature and confirmed by my life experiences suggested that as a black individual in the institutional context I did not matter at all to whites as a human being who has needs to be met in the world of work. How could this be when whites were so powerful and influential in *my* life? Where was the mutuality in our relationship? A standard normalised institutional practice of implicit and explicit black exclusion seemed to perpetuate the *status quo*.

The black experience

DoEAs do not form a significant group with any power in the British academy or society at the current stage of our evolvement as a group. In the congruently embedded institutional context of higher education power relations between the white majority and the DoEAs ensure the DoEAs are positioned as marginal. We exist as outsiders at the periphery of the organisation and society, aware of the contradictions of the laws which say one thing, and the psychological mindset of whites which says another – as indicated in Wells and Jennings US model. This positioning compounds the silent demand for DoEAs like myself to be seen to have taken on the cultural capital of the host society in order to hold onto our positions within the institution. This requires the denial of our history, group interest and background. Contradicting this denial and overtly acknowledging my interests met with white silence and angst. It also reinforces my role of token black in an institutional setting which is not designed to be responsive to my needs.

Given the fixedness of my positioning in relation to whites and my perceived marginality I feel vulnerable and highly expendable. The outcome of this token and marginal positioning is that whether from an organisational or identity position my relationship to whites is not negotiable: I must be glad for what I have been given (as opposed to merit) as the vignettes of my life reveal. It is expected that I know my predetermined place in society, and not make waves by raising the subject of race as an issue. Fernando (1996) lists the dilemmas that black people face when working in white organisations: lower paid positions, less legitimate power within the institution; being required to adopt restrictive organisational cultures and behavioural styles and having the responsibility for raising issues of race. In addition black professionals are unlikely to be able to support black clients/service users, as was seen in my case with the student in the vignettes, if they have taken on the cultural capital of society in order to gain their position. This disempowers black clients or users whose expectations of a culturally sensitive response to their needs is unmet by such black professionals. The black-white divide is therefore embedded in the organisational context and, according to Dickens and Dickens, must be worked around by the black individual achieving personal mastery, where possible. This strategy is in line with how ethnic minorities, as opposed to blacks, operate in British society.

Thomas' (1989) observation of organisations as the seat of irrational life provides further insights. Thomas observes that people's unconscious hopes and fears, the dreams and myths they live by and the history embedded in them influence their actions and relationships in the organisational context. In the case of the DoEAs Thomas further observes that the history of slavery and its chronic aftershocks undergird negative black-white relationships. He argues that we are still living in the aftermath of a social earthquake: slavery and its sequelae's long-term effects on racial identity, black self-esteem and white prejudice lie deep within our culture. Thomas points out that since equal opportunity policies and practices cannot eliminate these inner silenced experiences the means of fostering authentic collaboration must be found.

Subordinated members of the British family

Hill Collins (2001) adds another piece to the jigsaw by claiming that the DoEAs are accepted as subordinated member of the white family unlike other ethnic groups who are perceived as 'foreigners'. This suggests the conscious or unconscious co-option of blacks into British and American cultures to manage the legacy of empire. Continental Africans belong to a distinct and separate ethnic family into which they are born, even if under colonisation. So, although blacks, as the DoEAs, might seek to identify with Africans as a means of reweaving the bonds that were broken by slavery and colonisation, Africans do not necessarily identify with them. For the DoEAs to be born into British culture is to develop an inbuilt association with whites. In this way blacks are socialised to look up to whites as a fundamental component of their cultural conditioning. This must of necessity affect the perceptual salience of blacks and whites in relation to one another, a point that is developed further in later chapters.

The impact of the black experience on black employees

Researching from her psychotherapy practice in the UK, Alleyne (2004) notes that it is repeatedly observed that black workers are suffering significantly more negative and damaging effects of workplace stress and trauma than white workers. She describes this as workplace oppression and differentiates it from other workplace conflicts. She describes an internal and external cycle of events in which black workers feel ground down and trapped in the organisational context. Alleyne does this by contributing to understanding of a process she calls stigmatic stress and the cycle within which black workers can become trapped. This occurs when systematic micro- and macro-aggression results in stigmatic stress, causing the individual to experience shame and hurt. This shame and hurt becomes anticipated and re-experienced in each interaction and its persistence makes individuals adopt protective and defensive postures and attitudes in self-protection.

Alleyne theorises that over time as the culture of stigmatic stress becomes more established a wounding of self occurs with the experience of possible trauma. The person's work is badly affected: slip-ups and mistakes are made. When management reacts negatively to such slip-ups, black workers can experience feelings of unfairness, harassment and victimisation. When they are also given formal warnings or face disciplinary procedures black workers are likely to engage in ego justification in reaction against the perception of being devalued. Over time black workers in such situations may become pre-occupied with the white other and with fear of emotional collapse. When this is compounded by punitive attitudes from management workers enter into a fight/flight response resulting in illness manifested by erratic or long periods of sickness. This can create an *impasse* leading to post-traumatic stress and depression. White managers may respond defensively to charges of racism. A crisis ensues forcing the black employee to choose between either an employment tribunal or being resigned to the *status quo* or moving jobs.

Alleyne (2004) observes that many black respondents managed their work difficulties in similar ways: they tended to wait to be given opportunities and openings, as appropriate to black socialisation in their organisations. They seemed to want permission to be proactive: they may have lacked a sense of entitlement or felt dependent on whites. Alleyne acknowledges that the recurrence of these themes in their stories highlights their difficulties with issues of personal rights, entitlement and self-actualisation. This is seen as a consequence of the black socialisation to which they are subjected which is not about entitlement. This is evident in the vignettes I have shared and fits with the failure of organisations to use inter-group theory as well as the practice of neopigmentocracies. A review by the Sainsbury's Centre for Mental Health (SCMH, 2002) identifies the circle of fear that exists between the DoEAs and mental health professionals which means that they receive poor service provision. The SCMH review also asserts that if we combine the inequalities and disparities black people face in society with those embedded in the mental health service we are left with a rather bleak picture. Alleyne's work is supported by the idea of racism as a disease (Skillings and Dobbins, 1991) and poison (Goldberg and Hodes, 1992). Burke (1986) refers to blacks living with 'low level depression' as a constant. Smith (1976) finds it highly significant that their educational level is little related to earnings among the minority groups. Whereas whites earn substantially more the better educated they are the same is not true for blacks.

Reconceptualising black coping strategies

There is evidence that black academics seek to reframe the black experience to avoid the stigmatisation of the black identity. For example Alfred (1997) refutes Stonequist's (1961) contention that wherever there are cultural transitions and cultural conflicts, there will be marginal beings with dual personalities or double consciousnesses. Stonequist sees this dual personality as especially problematic for blacks (DoEAs) because blacks do not have a traditional culture of their own but are forced to express themselves in the only culture they know – that of whites. He argues that the consequences for blacks are that their efforts to improve themselves require them to become more like the whites and not to differentiate themselves. Blacks are trapped into attempts at equalling whites to demonstrate their ability and refute the stigma of inferiority. Stonequist delivers a blow: by blacks striving to equal themselves with whites, they throw themselves into a marginal status. According to Stonequist the advanced and educated blacks suffer most acutely from feelings of marginality.

Alfred (1997) suggests otherwise. She argues that the marginality of blacks should be understood as a 'creative marginality' better understood and described by black women themselves as the 'outsider within'. Lacey (2004) takes up the same theme using the term 'strategic assimilation' to describe how black women find a place for themselves within organisations and society.

Increasing autobiographical awareness

At the same time as carrying out this literature review I also followed through my action research commitment to share publicly the findings of my MBA research (Bravette, 1993): *Unleashing Human Potential: Black Women Managers and Emancipatory Action Research* at the Third World Congress for Action Research, Action Learning and Process Management at the University of Bath (Bravette, 1994). At this point I was still using my married name of Bravette. The findings were:

- What I had internalised as being personal was in fact highly political, in line with what the literature reveals

- There are strong social forces requiring me to be silent about the issues, to repress them – which made them even more political. This idea resonates with Matsuura's (2004) acknowledgment of the silence that surrounds African slavery as part of human experience

- I was in deep trouble, as were the majority of women in the action research group I had formed, as I came to realise that the issues were deep and complex and that we didn't necessarily have the knowledge and skills for working them through on our own. We lacked what I've termed 'bicultural competence' or cultural literacy. I decided to work on developing my own bicultural competence so that I could become a healing helper for others (Bravette, 1997).

At the point of carrying out my MBA research I was situated in the uncon-sciousness quadrants of the bicultural competence matrix and was largely unaware of the insights contained in the vignettes and the literature. At this point I struggled with racial experiences as isolated incidents. However, what I witnessed in the MBA group was black women battling to survive in white organisations aware of our blackness in the context of work but simul-taneously attempting to avoid and deny it, as it was denied and avoided by the white majority. This was necessary to ensure our survival. It became evi-dent that for black people race was a salient issue whereas for the white majority it was a taboo subject where cross-racial dialogue is concerned. This created a strong external force for silence on the subject of race which amounts to cultural censorship. As black women we had all internalised the awareness that to mention race as an issue in the workplace was to blight our possibilities of developing a career path, so we all adhered to the race taboo. Some of us were more aware of the political issues surrounding our blackness than others but no one was free of its ramifications.

Grouping for support with other black people in the workplace was not seen as a viable option because of the sense of fear and threat. This was why there was a need for a group such as the one I started outside of the workplace. Paradoxically, as women most of our lives were also too busy to allow us to meet regularly outside of work time! The possibility that it was the race taboo at work which was provoking anxiety about reflecting on and surfacing race as an issue and how this would impact on our subsequent ability to manage ourselves in the workplace should not be ruled out. Apart from one con-tinental African woman, those of us of African-Caribbean – DoEA – origin were overtly struggling with our race without any authentic life-enhancing strategies for managing the dynamics of this phenomenon. I concluded that it would be necessary for us as black women to come to terms with that in-heritance and heritage, to understand what it meant to be black, before we could effectively negotiate the white cultures of our workplaces. We were all attempting to do this ineffectively.

An important piece of tacit knowledge, which I began to note tentatively, was that although we are British in terms of socialisation this is rarely acknow-ledged. Our response to white racism is to reject our identification with whites and with the culture that nurtures and protects this racism. Through-out my research this insight became transparent as I came to understand how the white majority in Britain were effectively maintaining a strong social distance boundary line between themselves and their former slaves and colonised subjects by maintaining a social distance between themselves and us as blacks. We were negotiating 'white culture' and life in Britain with blindfolds over our eyes and had no hope of success until they were removed. But we dared not remove the blindfolds ourselves if we were to ensure our survival and jobs because of our dependency on whites.

As my autobiographical awareness grew however I began to see the systemic effects of the black workers experience: we were trapped in an ongoing black socialisation process that was taking place in the moment beyond our conscious level of awareness. The research had confirmed my understanding of black unconsciousness especially of unconscious bicultural competence, by which we understood the issues at a tacit level but kept them blocked in order to survive. We knew what the underlying issues were but given the marginality of our status as stigmatised DoEAs in organisational life which was rarely overtly acknowledged, we had unconsciously opted for collusion and complicity as opposed to authenticity and integrity. We had chosen survival not authenticity. The people who are unconsciously biculturally incompetent are our young people and we as parents are like walking zombies leading the naïve and uninitiated. Britain still has to confront the challenge of how to take care of not only its own young but also the young of its former slaves and colonised people.

In terms of my own biography, negative racial experiences in childhood and young adulthood were being reconfirmed in adulthood and lessons were being inadvertently transmitted to our young about what it means to be black in Britain. Both blacks and whites were shaping the consciousness of young blacks and keeping them in a predetermined place which maintained social distance between blacks and whites. Nowhere was the outcome of the systemic effects of the normalisation of the stigmatised black identity seen more clearly than in the life experiences of the young of this group: underachievement in the education system, exclusions, high levels of unemployment, drug and gun related crimes. These characteristics were underpinned by disillusionment and alienation from their elders who in their eyes seem to have sold out to a system that disadvantages them. Added to this, the ongoing societal liturgy of young black people without role models was working to lower their sense of self-worth and self-esteem further. My efforts to be an effective role model were being thwarted by my institutional experiences: my children are reluctant to make the choices I have made with so few outcomes.

Generational implications

Realising that my experience in the workplace would have implications for coming generations encouraged me to look at the education system and the role it plays in black inequality. Troyna (1988) points to the fact that colonialism and slavery were '... secured and justified by the belief in racial inferiority and inequality, a belief which has remained firmly embedded in the collective consciousness of the indigenous white UK population ...'. This completely coheres with my experience of living in Britain. Cashmore (1988) argues that the persistence of the colonial and slavery legacies ensured that my dreams of things being better for second and third generation DoEAs were false optimism. The disadvantages experienced by this group in the UK are only tenuously related to their newness in the society and are unlikely to diminish with the passage of time. Cashmore argues: '... it is precisely because their disadvantaged positions were likely to be reproduced in the life patterns of their children that distinguish colonial migrants from the experience of other migrant workers'. If the children of colonial migrants continue to occupy subordinate positions in the labour market, earn less than whites and are more vulnerable to the risk of unemployment, what were the implications for the DoEAs? Nor is this trend attributable in any significant measure to their apparent underachievement at school. The proposition that even in the midst of a severe recession school leavers of equal merit stand an equal chance of getting a job simply cannot be sustained. Young unemployed blacks tend to be better qualified than their white unemployed peers.

What are the reproducing forces? Ogbu (1991) and Cummins (1986) concur with Cashmore (1988). They suggest that the past experience of the migrant group in an alien society and culture determine whether they will be successful or not in their achievements. All these scholars agree that academic performance problems are due to complex forces not only in schools and classrooms but also in broader historical, economic and socio-cultural domains. Of interest here is their classification of minority groups: caste-like or involuntary minorities – those people who were originally brought into the society involuntarily through slavery, conquest or colonisation. Thereafter these minorities find themselves relegated to menial positions and denied true assimilation into the mainstream of society. Involuntary minorities or non-immigrants usually experience more difficulties with social adjustment and academic achievement in school. This finding is of particular importance when related to the experience of the DoEAs and the continuum of races which places the DoEAs on the bottom rung.

Doing my Master's research, doctoral research and working with the issues in the University, and which many of our learners and colleagues refer to as a 'black university' had brought me to a realisation that I needed to develop my conscious bicultural competence using self-re-education. I was aware of my lack of historical and racial consciousness and how this had been compounded by my determination to fit into mainstream white society. Pryce's (1979) 'mainliner' classification of West Indians and the attitudes and values they adopt when living in the UK closely matched my own experiences, no doubt influenced by the fact that I had been 'peer-proofed' when I was separated as 'bright' from being with my black counterparts in the school system (Fordham, 1991). Pryce describes mainliners as follows:

> Mainliners are more concerned, on the whole, with adhering to the official line of thinking on all matters relating to immigrants than with articulating a black-orientated viewpoint of their own. They are also the most law-abiding, the least militant and the most conformist element in the black community.

Based on his studies of West Indians living in Bristol, Pryce explores what he terms the 'psychic disorientation and confusion' of West Indians in white society. I identified most with his statement that for black British young people:

> The school anglicises [her] installing in [her] psyche a preference for all the 'white' values of the dominant society, yet that society continually defines [her] as inferior, and [she] can never seem to measure up to it. [She] seems destined to remain an outsider by the very same values that she has been taught to revere.

What should I, as an academic and educator, do with the knowledge I was developing? I was faced with the challenge of making the action turn, of integrating inquiry and practice explicitly and implicitly in my everyday conduct. This was so that I could extricate myself from the 'endless pressure' found by Ken Pryce (1979) to frame the life experience of the DoEAs as we struggle to meet the demands of being 'good enough' which we perceive are being placed on us by whites.

Awareness and choice – conscious bicultural competence

I was additionally challenged by Byrne's (1978) reason for not including a discussion of academic women in her book on women and education. She argues that such women are 'best qualified to fight for their own equality'. This left me wondering about my own responsibilities as a black woman in academia. Many of us leave the institutions rather than stay and engage with the inevitable struggle. This is despite the fact that we place our children at the frontline of the struggle in schools. I was now at a choice point: over the years I had experienced extreme dissonance in presenting the dominant view of 'organisational behaviour' whilst conforming to being culturally conditioned. This has been especially the case when it includes a view that there is equality of opportunity when I know full well that sexism and racism is rife in our society. I experienced dissonance between teaching students who are the DoEAs and raising their aspirations towards a goal they were unlikely to achieve in any significant numbers. I also experienced dissonance as a DoEA myself in higher education: I am generally perceived by all and sundry as a token black. Deciding to face up to the issue of race was certainly not an easy option, nor was it a non-political decision.

Luz Reyes and Halcon (1988) discuss racism in academia and the obstacles to be overcome in identifying covert racism as the most pervasive form in higher education. Moghissi's (1994) interesting observations about the experience of racism in the academy resonates strongly with my own experiences. Acker (1994) notes: 'there is a near silence about 'race' and ethnicity in terms of their impact on British academic women'. I made the decision that my research should contribute towards breaking the silence around race, speaking as a 'black' woman of African-Caribbean descent with experiences spanning the time period of 'mass immigration' of African-Caribbeans to the UK in the 1950s.

Generative educators

For us as educators and therefore cultural practitioners this and the previous chapter raises a number of issues about British culture and its differential socialisation processes in terms of what is happening to black children in British society. More often than not the problems black children experience in the society are seen as a dysfunction of the black community. The vignettes and the literature suggest otherwise – that we are looking at a societal problem. What does this mean for us as cultural practitioners responsible for educating our young? There are clear indicators to suggest that black parents need to urgently reassess the role we have to play in educating our own children. It is also apparent that educators in the formal system play an important role. More importantly, there is a wall of silence and ignorance that needs to be broken down and the task has been left to us as the DoEAs and the DoSOs. My approach is based on Gandhi's famous edict: be the change you want to see. In the next chapter I go backwards in time to gain an historical perspective on the black experience in the UK in terms of what underpins the silence, unawareness and denial.

4

Historical perspectives

To discover our history is to discover our somethingness (beingness) before
someone else created us. To come to know ourselves as we were prior to our recreation by alien means we will be in charge of our own becoming, the creators of
our own consciousness, the creation of ourselves as namers of the world, the
namers of ourselves which gives us the power of self-determination and self-
direction. (Wilson, 1993:52)

To rediscover one's history is not only an act of self-discovery; it is an act of self-
creation – a resurrection from the dead, a tearing away of the veil, a revelation of
the mystery. (Wilson, 1993)

(Black people) have a responsibility to describe the world from the position they
occupy – for other (black people); and for (white people), who will not know unless
they are informed. If we wish to describe and analyse human experience, and to
formulate explanations of the world which take human beings into account, then
we must include the experience and understandings of (black people)
...(paraphrased ('black' replaces 'women') from Spender, 1988).

We have suffered as much as any group in human history, and if this suffering
has ennobled us, it has also wounded us and pushed us into defensive strategies
that are often self-defeating. But we haven't fully admitted this to ourselves. The
psychological realm is murky, frightening and just plain embarrassing. And a risk
is involved in exploring it: the risk of discovering the ways in which we contribute
to, if not create, the reality in which we live. Denial, avoidance, and repression
intervene to save us from this risk. But, of course, they only energise what is
oppressed with more and more negative power, so that we are victimised as
much by our own buried fears as by racism. (Steele, 1980)

Introduction

During the course of the mini-lectures and discussion forums facilitated during 2005 (Gordon, 2006) I suggested to black parents that we have a responsibility to work together with teachers in the school system to ensure that our children's needs are met where the legacy of slavery is concerned. For this we would need to approach teachers directly. I am not sure that any of these parents have been brave enough to do this given the silence that surrounds the issue. This chapter is important because of the insights it provides us as educators into understanding the historical background which underpins the experience outlined in earlier chapters. It also outlines the role we have to play in correcting the visible and invisible legacies that history has bequeathed us. The chapter is divided into three sections to allow engagement with the three geographical locations and cultures that have influenced the identity and personality formation of the DoEAs. These locations suggest that this group who are known, and refer to themselves, by a variety of names including blacks, black British, Afro-Caribbeans, African-Caribbeans, British Africans, West Indians and Caribbeans, are more correctly identified as British African-Caribbeans. The sections that follow provide an overview of the issues I found pertinent to understanding each context as I researched with the intention of gaining the self-knowledge that is critical to the development of conscious bicultural competence. Given the insights gained from the previous chapters, the research engaged with in this chapter and beyond grew increasingly threatening for me as I was now surfacing the tacit and hidden knowledge of the unconscious bicultural competence quadrant.

1. Africa

My research reveals that Africa and Africans had both been inferiorised in my mind as a result of my socialisation into British culture. My search for an African culture of origin in the early 1990s was the reactive turning away from a society that rejected me on account of my espoused race. The search eventually identified Kush (modern day Ethiopia) and Kemet (modern day Egypt) as important sites of the beginning of African civilisation and culture and also as major contributors to world civilisation as we know it today. This insight was gained after arduous study of historical texts, attendance at lectures and enrolment on a Global African Studies course to help me piece together the intricate jigsaw which confronted me in my search for my culture of origin. Interestingly, I found myself caught up in the arguments between two conflicting camps which ironically also represented the dual aspects of my heritage: Afrocentric scholars representing my African heritage and Western scholars representing my British heritage. I came to recognise that the Caribbean experience – and therefore slavery – has been largely eclipsed from serious study. This is important because in the Caribbean and North America Africans were recreated into 'blacks'. Ongoing debates about black under-achievement in British society are also largely silent about this experience.

The debate about the beginning of human civilisation and which groups have contributed to this process is important because of how the DoEAs have been positioned historically. It is also important if a clear perspective of history and the evolution of the human race, as seen in world history, is to be achieved. This is in order to understand and so refute the oft repeated untruths that black people are sub-humans or barbarians and the rest of the ideological argument developed and perpetuated to support the enslavement and in-human treatment of Africans as a group of people.

Slurs are inflicted daily on people of African descent and are typical of the remarks which mould the consciousness of both black and white peoples in contemporary society (Biko, 1996). All are from influential people who affect our thinking and consciousness whether through textbooks, popular media or the church:

> It will be seen that, when we classify Mankind by colour, the only primary race that has not made a creative contribution to any civilisation is the Black race. Arnold Toynbee, Historian, *A Study of History*, 1934.

> I am apt to suspect the Negroes ... to be naturally inferior to the White. There never was a civilised nation of any other complexion than white, nor even any individual eminent either in action or speculation. No ingenious manufacturers amongst them, no arts, no sciences. David Hume, Philosopher, *Essays and Treatises on Several Subjects*, London 1753 Vol. 1.

> We come among the Africans as members of a superior race and servants of a Government that desires to elevate the more degraded portions of the human family. Dr Livingstone, Doctor, Elspeth Huxley, *Livingstone*, 1974.

> Whites are more intelligent than Negroes; intelligence is overwhelmingly the result of genetic inheritance rather than environmental influences ... *The Saturday Review Magazine* (17 May 1969) quoting Arthur Jensen, a noted University of California psychologist.

There have been other white Europeans who have acknowledged the contri-bution made by African peoples to world civilisation. What they have said is in direct contradiction to the quotes above but is rarely heard in public circles. For example:

> There a people now forgotten discovered while others were yet barbarians, the ele-ments of the arts and sciences. A race of men now rejected for their black skin and woolly hair founded on the study of the laws of nature, those civil and religious

systems which still govern the universe. The author of these words was an eighteenth century French academician of the highest esteem in European academic circles, Count C F Volney writing in *Ruins of Empire* 1789 (Preface to the 1st edition).

The African continent is no recent discovery; it is not a new world like America or Australia ... while yet Europe was the home of wondering barbarians one of the most wonderful civilisations on record had began to work out its destiny on the banks of the Nile ... J A Rogers in *History of Nations*, Vol 18 (Africa's Gift to America) 1961.

The German scholar of history, Herr Eugen Georg declared:

A splendid era of black seems to have preceded all the later races! There must once have been a tremendous Negro expansion, since the original masters of all the lands between Iberia and the Cape of Good Hope and East India were primitive and probably dwarfed black men. We have long had proof that a primitive Negroid race of pigmies once lived around the Mediterranean. Blacks were the first to plow the mud of the Nile. *The Adventure of Mankind*, E P Dutton and Co, 1931.

It is now generally agreed that the first human being was from Africa and that African civilisation is one of the oldest, far older than that of Europe. Although Egypt is in the north of the African continent, because of its important position in the development of world civilisation as we know it today, the fact that it is African is denied by many European and North American historians. There is also disagreement among them over whether these Egyptians are Caucasians or Negroes.

Afrocentrism as a philosophy (Asante, 1992) looks at the world from the African standpoint. One of the fundamental claims made by Afrocentric scholars is that Greek civilisation is derived from Egypt where the ancient Egyptians were black (James, 1992). The focus of Afrocentrists is on Egypt rather than Ethiopia because the western world is claiming Egypt as theirs. Presumably no claims are made about Ethiopia because it is too far inland to the south. However, deeper study shows that there were civilisations in existence before Egypt which were in the south (ie deeper into Africa) and that these civilisations actually fed into Egypt (eg Kush, modern day Ethiopia) giving Egypt its civilisation.

Clarke (1986) quotes a white Professor, Bruce Williams, of the University of Chicago who wrote in 1980

the people in Nubia (sometimes called Kush) had an advanced political organisation hundreds of years before the first dynasty of Egypt, and what we think of as Egyptian civilisation may have moved from South to North – a concept which is contrary to current thinking on the subject.

This is not new information for African scholars but is likely to be given more credence when from the pen of a white professor.

Clarke (1986) argues that:

> If Egypt is a dilemma in Western historiography, it is a created dilemma. The Western historians, in most cases, have rested the foundation of what is called 'Western Civilisation' on the false assumptions, or claim, that the ancient Egyptians were white people. To do this they had to ignore great masterpieces on Egyptian history written by other white historians who did not support this point of view, such as Gerald Massey's great classic, *Ancient Egypt, The Light of the World* (1907), and his other works, *A Book of the Beginnings*, and *The Natural Genesis*. Other neglected works by white writers are *Politics, Intercourse, And Trade of The Carthaginians, Ethiopians, and Egyptians*, by A H L Heeren (1833), and *Ruins of Empires*, by Count Volney (1787).

The intra-psychic outcome

My most important finding from reviewing African history was making the link between the internal and external world of the individual. It is not necessary to pursue the discussion about Egypt's African roots as the evidence is available in history books. Acknowledging the existence of conflicting views is very important, however, as is being aware that without critical consciousness and an open mind it is possible to be easily misled or to find what you want to find. What both whites and blacks must understand is the similarity of the struggles occurring at macro levels (west versus south; black versus white) as well as at micro levels (black versus white; African versus Western aspects of oneself). Accordingly, I was pushed to ask myself the following questions:

- What is the western interest in denying Africa what is rightly hers (the legacy of Egypt and early African civilisation)?

- What is the western interest in denying the humanity of the DoEAs and inflicting on them the stamp of black inferiority?

Within the psyche:

- What is this British/western mindset/force that is antagonised and cannot rest beside the African/black aspect and which pushes the individual to make a choice for one aspect or the other? But never both because of the irreconcilable differences between the two?

- What is the British/western interest in silencing the African?

The challenge for us as educators is in how to work with these divisions in our own psyche if we are to avoid or overcome the double consciousness which DuBois recognised as early as 1903: the legacy of those who are forcibly split

49

between the two aspects of themselves, in the case of DoEAs: enslaved African and English and therefore, black and white. Phinney *et al* (1990) noted that for 'increasing numbers of people the conflicts are not between different groups but between different cultural values, attitudes, and expectations within themselves'. This is the bicultural challenge of integration or trans-formation.

In relation to the psychic disorientation, confusion and despair described in the previous chapters it was my lack of awareness of my own historical roots and the conflict between the two aspects of my heritage that had contributed to my existential crisis of meaning. I had had no teachers to facilitate my understanding of these issues. As my autobiographical awareness grew I be-came aware that it was my responsibility as a DoEA living in the African Dia-spora to make sense of my own past as an adult instead of expecting the white ethnic majority to educate members of my group about our history. They can only teach my history from their perspective and it may not serve their political interests to teach this history anyway. I had come upon two contra-dicting interpretations: Europe and North America versus Afrocentrists. This is despite both using the same data source. Gareth Morgan (1983) suggests that how we study an apple determines what results we get: one person might look at the apple, another might feel it whilst another might choose to chew it and all would get different results. The vast differences in opinion and the interpretation of facts which surfaced forced me to delve further for truth. The DoSOs have been telling their truth for some time now. But no counter-balancing black truth is being told and so the balance of the world is upset. Diop (1974) makes this historical challenge: 'the history of Africa will remain suspended in the air and cannot be written correctly until African historians connect it with the history of Egypt'.

This brief analysis of African history shows it to be contested terrain, and yet critical for accurate self-knowledge for both whites and blacks. The fact that black people learn British history from a white European perspective and not our own African perspective goes some way to explain our confusion and dis-location in the UK.

2. The Caribbean, the Slave Trade and Slavery

The present is where we get lost – if we forget our past and have no vision of the future. (Ayi Kwei Armah 1978)

In everlasting memory of the anguish of our ancestors
May those who died rest in peace
May those who return find their roots

May humanity never again perpetuate
Such injustice against humanity
We, the living, vow to uphold this.
Plaque at the entrance of Elimina 'Dungeons', Ghana.

Enslaved Africans were recreated into the image of sub-humans to justify en-slavement. Once slavery was abolished the DoEAs were left to fend for them-selves by slave owners and were forgotten, disowned, denied and discarded by Africans, their ethnic family. Engaging with African history helped me become aware of history as both a source of self-knowledge and mythology. In the same way that most of us as the DoEAs are unaware of the significance of history in terms of self-knowledge and as a means of shaping conscious-ness, we also know little about the details of the slave trade, the institution of slavery and its impact on us as a people. It is a subject avoided by the DoEAs and the ethnic majority alike.

The justification for African dehumanisation is evident in the hierarchical grading of mankind offered by J S Mill, a philosopher of British Liberalism, who argued that the English, the Continentals, the 'backward' races of Asia and the African 'savages' occupied successively lower rungs on the hierarchy of civilisation. The 'civilised' races had the mission of civilising the 'back-wards' and the 'savages' to the point where they could be treated as equals – as is claimed has been achieved through colonialism (Parekh, 2005).

The degrading form of slavery of the slave trade can be understood as an out-growth of British and European industrialisation and capitalism from the mid 15th to the 19th century. Europeans, especially the British, French and Por-tuguese, already had a presence in Africa before the slave trade which in-volved what Davidson describes as mutually beneficial trading and commer-cial partnerships with the Africans. The Portuguese were deeply involved in buying slave labour for the Americas well before either France or Britain. Britain, concerned to maintain her leading edge in industrialisation, simply used the connections it already had in Africa to get the slave trade off the ground. Britain's John Hawkins was one of the earliest slave traders.

Accounts vary about whether Africans captured Africans and sold them to the European traders or whether European traders raided villages and captured people. It is likely that both accounts have some truth. The rights and wrongs of this trade vary according to the interest and subjective experience of those who are giving the account. Records from the logs of the slave ships and sea-men's accounts (quoted in Davidson, 1991) such as contained in *Collections of Voyages and Travels* (Barbot and Churchill 1732) are informative. African men and women who had been enslaved were not necessarily docile as was usually depicted:

> ... we stood in arms, firing on the revolted slaves, of whom we killed some, and wounded many ... and many of the most mutinous, leapt over board, and drown'd themselves in the ocean with much resolution, shewing no manner of concern for life.

Not all the peoples on the African continent lived in societies which were as highly developed as Egypt, Mali and Songhay. Europeans are said to have used the least developed people to typify African savagery thus supporting their claims for African inferiority.

The reality of the Slave Trade

The slave trade is often talked about as no more than statistics. The reality of the slave trade was immense in its impact on the lives of men, women and children, whole families and communities, nations and a continent. African men and women were dispersed across the globe as slaves. Visiting the slave dungeons in Elmina, Ghana in July 1996 moved me as a Diasporic African and human being closer to understanding the deep-seated nature of the trauma endured by my ancestors. The ocean was rough when we visited and it was as if the remains of our ancestors were calling out to us, even as we thought of the many Africans who had chosen to die by drowning themselves rather than become slaves. Acknowledging the pain of the experience some days later I recalled Bennet's (1985) account of the slave trade:

> The slave trade was people living, lying, stealing, murdering, dying. The slave trade was a black man who stepped out of his house for a breath of fresh air and ended up, ten months later, in Georgia with bruises on his back and a brand on his chest.

> The slave trade was a black mother suffocating her newborn baby because she didn't want him to grow up a slave.

> The slave trade was a 'kind' captain forcing his suicide minded passengers to eat by breaking their teeth, though, as he said, he was 'naturally compassionate'.

> The slave trade was a bishop sitting on an ivory chair on a wharf in the Congo and extending his fat hand in wholesale baptism of slaves who were rowed beneath him, going in chains to the slave ships.

> The slave trade was a greedy king raiding his own villages to get slaves to buy brandy.

> The slave trade was a pious captain holding prayer services twice a day on his slave ship and writing later the famous hymn 'How Sweet the Name of Jesus Sounds'.

The slave trade was deserted villages, bleached bones on slave trails and people with no last names. It was Caesar Negro, Angelo Negro and Negro Mary... (pp29-30)

The figure of just how many Africans has been lost to the African continent as a result of the slave trade continues to be contested between DoEAs and DoSOs. I can't help but reflect on the outrage expressed about the six million Jews who were systematically exterminated by the Nazis. Yet millions of Africans were enslaved, with significant numbers dying in the 'middle passage' and such indifference and silence. Those who survived the journey to the Caribbean and the Americas were deprived of their homeland, their families, their culture, their religion, their everything as the slave masters split families, separated men and women, pitted them against one another: 'house niggers' versus 'field niggers' and conditioned them into accepting and believing in their slave status.

What about my own personal process in all this? The research for this account of slavery was tremendously painful, including my visit to Ghana in July of 1996 and the slave dungeons in what Westerners call 'castles'. I felt that I came face to face with the pain that had been dogging me for so long. Jung's concept of the 'collective unconscious' was to find new meaning for me. In the dungeons I realised that only because 'my ancestors were that I am' and yet they remained largely forgotten as I learn about the ancestors of Europeans in the British school system! Some (1994) has written about the need to find balance between the dead and the living in one's group because only in so doing we can heal ourselves. All this flooded through me as I stood in the dark dank dungeon, unpleasant but deodorised and prettified for tourists.

Two Ghanaian women relived the scenes of our ancestors' capture for our benefit by wailing in high plaintive tones for the life of the loved ones they had lost. We were all women in the women's dungeons, our lighted candles dangerously balanced, wax dripping onto our hands and clothes, some of us with tears streaming down our faces, others numb with shock. Standing there we acknowledged within ourselves that this was the point of our departure – this very dungeon. We all experienced the pain of that collective unconscious and many of us suddenly realised why we had come to Ghana, even though we had been uncertain when we booked our flights. Kemp (1995) an African-American gives a descriptive account of her experience, which echoes my own:

As we crowded into the dungeons, we shivered in the cold damp tombs where millions of slaves were crammed, sometimes for months, waiting to be taken on a journey of no return. We stood on the floor of the dungeons, now eight inches higher than when they were built due to the tons of compacted excrement and exfoliated skin cells from the bodies of slaves. In the women's chambers, we saw staircases leading to the Dutch and English sailors' quarters where young African girls were taken. And afterwards, as we crossed the yard that led to the male dungeons, we glimpsed the shores that were the last sight of home for Africans who might have been our fore-parents.

On entering the male dungeons a middle-aged woman suddenly collapsed, overcome by emotion. Others, holding torches, sat quietly beside her on the dungeon floor. Several of us inclined our heads as if listening for voices. Everyone cried.

Like Kemp we were the recipients of a moving speech in which as Diasporic Africans we were asked for forgiveness by the Ghanaian chiefs on behalf of our ancestors who had been guilty of selling us into slavery. This was important because this fact is regularly and defensively used against us by white people in Britain to remind us that it was not only the Europeans who were responsible for slavery. The knowledge of having been betrayed by our own people has further deepened the vacuum already deep within us.

Post-traumatic slavery syndrome

In concluding this most painful of episodes of our history the work of Leary (2005) contributes to understanding of the impact of slavery on the DoEAs today. Leary uses post-traumatic stress syndrome theory in a collective way, applying it to the DoEAs as a group as it has been applied to indigenous peoples or Jewish Holocaust survivors who also suffered historical injuries. She contends that the DoEAs continue to be badly affected by past centuries of slavery because the original enslaved Africans were never treated for the severe trauma of being degraded, beaten and abused, seeing relatives whipped, raped and killed, being forced to breed and having their babies taken from them, and all the other unspeakable things that occurred during slavery. Patterson (1973) and Hiro (1971) also offer important insights into this experience and the consequences for the modern DoEAs. Even after slavery officially ended, nothing was done to enable recovery from the trauma it had caused. Leary maintains that the traumatising circumstances continued and even increased because of the treatment that has kept blacks in bondage. Blacks across the world still face racism, oppression and societal inequality without ever having had the opportunity to heal from the injuries of slavery.

Leary stresses that people don't have to be direct victims of a horrible occurrence to be traumatised by it as seen in the example of the attacks on the World Trade Centre and Pentagon. People across the US were traumatised even though they were nowhere near the attacks. Attitudes and behaviours resulting from trauma can be unconsciously passed down from generation to generation. This can be seen in the survival techniques developed during slavery which have been carried down the generations even when they are no longer needed to the detriment of the black community. This alone indicates that important remedial work needs to be done with this group.

Colonisation: just another name for continued slavery?

Although the slavery was officially abolished in 1834 it took many more years before physical slavery actually ended and colonisation took over. The impact of colonisation must be considered in this context also because of the effect it still has on Africa and Africans, even in the Diaspora, particularly in the form of neo-colonialism. Colonisation occurs where a country's native population is subjugated by a conquering colonising group as well as when Africans are turned into slaves on plantations in British colonies. For the British colonisation of their slave plantations was the natural next step after abolition. Industrial nations found it necessary to colonise in order to exploit the resources of the colonies. This competition for industrial might between European nations led to a scramble over Africa which still continues today. A study of how Europe has been developed through industrialisation, capitalism, colonisation and imperialism demonstrates how Africa was simultaneously underdeveloped (Rodney, 1989).

Williams (1987:249) gives an African perspective of the process:

> The new masters of the continent were in the position of all-power and could, therefore, make their viewpoints the viewpoints of the world. The system of reducing Blacks to non-persons was so thoroughgoing that not only did the various people of the world regard them as such, but – tragedy of tragedies – the Blacks themselves came to feel inferior and to hate themselves and all of their kind.

Language and Culture

Over time and as a result of their degradation enslaved Africans began to accept their lower status as their natural lot in life. Implicit to slavery in the Caribbean and colonisation in Africa has been the imposition of the British language and culture. Ngugi (1987) describes how as a child living in Kenya he had to pass six subjects ranging from Maths to Nature Study and Kiswahili in order to gain entrance to secondary school. All the papers were written in English:

> Nobody could pass the exam who failed the English Language paper no matter how brilliantly he had done in the other subjects. I remember one boy in my class of 1954 who had distinctions in all subjects except English, which he had failed. He was made to fail the entire exam ... English was the official vehicle and the magic formula to colonial elitedom. (p12)

English is still the official language of those African former British colonies. The official languages of Africa still include English, Arabic, French and Portuguese. Many of us have recognised that we did not escape the impact of colonisation because the language which Ngugi describes as 'the carrier of culture' had colonised our minds. Bob Marley in Redemption Song enjoins us to 'free ourselves from mental slavery; nobody but ourselves can free our minds'. We find ourselves bound to England and its culture through the language we speak. Ngugi suggests that '... language as culture is thus mediating between me and my own self; between my own self and other selves; between me and nature. Language is mediating in my very being'. Sivanandan (1974) writes about 'alien gods gone astray' in our flesh. This separation from self for the DoEAs has been a major outcome of enslavement and colonisation and continues to keep the DoEAs as people who are mentally colonised even if the physical chains have been removed.

The important point to understand is that colonial and imperial regimes imposed pseudo speciation and negative identities which prevent the widespread acquisition of strengths of character in blacks that can resist authoritarian solutions to pressing social problems. Davidson (1991) points out that colonialism in Africa effectively arrested the transition from traditional to modern forms of economic and political relations.

3. Life in Britain: The DoEAs in the UK
Arrival: social and public policy issues
Although DoEAs have been in Britain since at least the sixteenth century, we only began to migrate to Britain in significant numbers from 1945 onwards. Unlike America, Britain operated her slavery outside the metropolis and this has important implications for her relationship with blacks today especially in terms of 'white absenteeism' (Patterson, 1973). Importantly, many of these former African men and women who had been enslaved had been removed from their 'culture of origin' so that the name 'African' became like a curse – and they would aspire to the colonial culture of power. Numerous reasons are given for this mass migration:

- black workers and soldiers had arrived earlier from the colonies to fight in the British army or to help with the war effort

- Britain needed the cheap labour and the ex-colonised would accept low wages to rebuild their post-war economy

- dearth of job opportunities in the colonies depleted by colonisers

- an opportunity to visit the 'Motherland'

■ the hurricane which struck Jamaica in 1951 sparked off a great migratory movement. At that time, Commonwealth citizens were allowed free entry under the British Nationality Act of 1948.

Solomos (1993) notes that, contrary to popular depiction, most of the migrants arriving in Britain between 1945 and 1954 were there because of government initiatives and were from other European countries. This point is made to highlight the encouragement given to this group compared with government concern over the social and political consequences of the relatively small-scale migration from the colonies during this period. We are led to believe that the 1950s was an age of innocence when the British government understood little about black immigration but Solomos argues otherwise:

> Throughout the period an increasingly racialised debate about immigration took place, focusing on the supposed 'social problems' of having too many black immigrants and the question of how they could be stopped from entering given their legal rights following the 1948 British Nationality Act.

It seems that the familiar clip of the Empire Windrush arriving in 1948 with its 417 passengers obscured the fact that the majority of immigrants continued to come from the Irish Republic, Europe and white Commonwealth countries. Carter, Harris and Joshi's (1987) research shows that by 1952 both the Labour and Conservative administrations had instituted a number of covert and sometimes illegal administrative measures to discourage black immigration. It is argued that a deliberate *laissez faire* policy on immigration that failed to tackle racism had predictable consequences but Solomos disputes the idea of a laissez faire policy in relation to black immigration. Rather he argues:

> ... it was one of intense debate within government departments and in public circles about the impact of black immigration on housing, the welfare state, crime and other social problems. ... these debates ... were also about the effect of black immigration on the 'racial character of the British people' and on the national identity. (p59)

That these Caribbean islands were also Britain's ex-colonies and slave plantations is rarely discussed in the literature. This had important implications because the history of the DoEAs had been tied up with Britain's for the past several hundred years. Some of them, or their parents, had even fought in its defence. Many had been encouraged to think of Britain as their mother country, perhaps by missionaries and saw their arrival in the UK as the fulfilment of a dream and probably the exercise of their right. Britain had materially benefited from its colonies: slavery, the plantation economy and the captive colonial market for her products had greatly helped Britain's industrialisation. With the economic boom which Britain was experiencing and no white labour force able or willing to do menial work, Britain naturally looked back to the now redundant labour force they had left behind in the colonies. Blacks entered Britain as non-immigrants or as an involuntary minority, as discussed in chapter four. Independence from British rule for the former colonies had not meant financial independence nor had the legacy of slavery gone from the minds of the European, no matter how emancipated the former slaves felt. This was the basis for the growth of a disparate psychological contract between members of the two groups.

Many DoEAs came to the UK with no intention of staying. They came to make money in the hope of returning home to their families in the Caribbean. Financial gain and the possibility of gaining some education were powerful incentives. Although racially unpleasant, life was financially more rewarding than remaining unemployed in the West Indies. Richmond (1954) gives insight into the employment situation in the West Indies based on facts drawn from official reports and qualitative data from the men's experiences and quotes men who were repatriated back to the West Indies in 1943:

> I should have written to you before now as promised, but after the shock of existing conditions here it's a wonder I am capable of writing at all; to be quite frank I really expected things to be bad, but not in my wildest dreams could I imagine anything as bad. ... (p.142)

Richmond notes that the situation in the West Indies was comparable only with 'the chaos in this country after the first world war, which the government in England was determined not to repeat'. Because of reports like these, many who might have left Britain decided to stay and others who had been repatriated worked their way back. Many also paid their own fares to come and seek opportunities.

As black people our parents were subjected to racial abuse. Colour bars were common in pubs, dance halls and other public places. Building societies, estate agents, employers and local authorities discriminated against them, forcing them to move into disadvantaged areas where their presence strained resources. Our parents were segregated in places of work and found themselves concentrated in certain industries or on night shifts where they scarcely came into contact with white workers. They took up dirty or low paid jobs, were generally the first to be declared redundant and were unlikely to be promoted: this still continues today. As early as 1954 Richmond concludes his study: 'Whatever the result of further research may be, the present study conclusively demonstrates that there is widespread colour prejudice in Britain'. This prejudice was to culminate in what was claimed to be white working-class resentment of our presence, which eventually erupted into incidents such as the race riots in Nottingham and Notting Hill in 1958 when Teddy Boys went 'nigger-hunting' with knives and iron pipes.

The race riots of 1958 shocked public opinion and required an explanation and an answer. I arrived in the UK in 1959 in this climate of racial intolerance. The passage of the 1962 Commonwealth Immigrants Act indicated that the prevalent image of 'coloured colonials' as men and women of inferior and un-assimilatable racial stock had been accepted and that they were inherently undesirable. This reinforced Britain's conception of itself as a basically fair and tolerant society. The prevailing view was that the uncharacteristic demonstrations of intolerance had been provoked by the immigrants them-selves who had taken unfair advantage of a generous open-door policy and arrived in excessive numbers. Shifting the responsibility for the black predica-ment from the government and white society to black people absolved the government from the need to develop coherent and positive policies and placated public opinion. It has also had long term consequences.

The 1962 Commonwealth Immigrants Act did not end the debate. The Act was acknowledged to be a colour bar. 1968 heard Powell's infamous rivers of blood speech:

> As I look ahead, I am filled with foreboding. Like the Roman, I seem to see 'the River Tiber foaming with much blood'. The tragic and intractable phenomenon which we watch with horror on the other side of the Atlantic, but which there is interwoven with the history and existence of the States itself, is coming upon us here by own volition and our own neglect. (*The Observer* 21 April, 1968)

1969 saw the introduction of the Immigration Appeals Act by Labour and the 1971 Immigration Act by the Conservative Government. An analysis of poli-tical discourse shows how the government and particularly the media were responsible for problematising black people (van Dijk, 1993).

Internal colonisation?
Blauner's (1972) concept of 'internal' colonisation, whereby minority groups in white societies under bureaucratic white control are no more than 'inter-nally colonised groups', is another important development. The particular features of such internally colonised groups are:

- they are forcibly made to exist in a society that is not their own
- they are so subjugated that their social mobility is limited and their political involvement restricted
- their own culture is deprecated or even extinguished

The outcome, according to Blauner's analysis, is that the colonised group becomes trapped in a caste-like situation which affects the group's self-conception. It accepts the 'superiority' of the colonising group and views itself as inferior (Cashmore, 1988; van Dijk, 1993).

The black experience in Britain

In her study of Jamaicans in the UK Foner (1977) says about blackness:

> The fact that black skin is more of a stigma in England does not mean, of course, that it was not a stigma back home. Black skin has long been devalued in Jamaica. This stems from Jamaica's history as a plantation colony based on African slavery. Whites were, in the days of slavery, masters, and throughout the colonial period, rulers. Indeed a white bias has permeated the entire society since the eighteenth century: in the eyes of most Jamaicans, white stands for wealth, privilege, and power. (p129)

She adds:

> The colour-class hierarchy in Jamaica is a three-tiered one, and it is marked by a high degree of shade consciousness ... whites ... belong to the upper class, people of colour to the middle (the result of black and white liaisons) and blacks to the lowest class. (p130)

Of their experience in England she writes:

> Whatever their shade and whatever their achievements, Jamaicans in England tend to be viewed as lower class and inferior by most English people. (p131)

> It is not surprising that Jamaicans in England are constantly aware of being black. On the bus, in the shops, and on the job, they can never forget that to English people their black skin marks them off as 'something less than human'. (p133)

My initial hypothesis was that the problems faced by us as the DoEAs would eventually sort themselves out. After all it was only 40 years since the 'mass immigration' of the 1950s. Was the newness of our presence in Britain the cause of our negative experiences? But my hypothesis was totally negated by these research findings. The issues were much greater than mere xenophobia and were related to identity foreclosure due to the imposition of black culture (Marcia, 1966).

What becomes evident through this brief traverse through history is the changing discourse which hides the private reality of a continuing master-slave relationship between the DoEAs and the DoSOs. In Britain the DoEAs are referred to as immigrants like any other immigrant from Europe which blurs the embedded nature of this relationship.

History as a source of self-knowledge

Coming to the understanding that it is history that creates a shared identity in a people by reminding them of what happened to them in the past and that in Britain I had to repress my history because of its intimate relationship with British history came as a shock. Immersed in history that has been taught by the ethnic majority, I had been denied the gift and legacy of self-knowledge. My history as a DoEA merged with that of Britain and became submerged and repressed under romanticised interpretations of colonialism and the benefits perceived to have been brought by the colonisers to the colonised (Ferguson, 2004) while little is acknowledged about the enslaved. The legacies of slavery and colonisation were embedded through socialisation into British culture. Understanding my history at this stage of my life enabled me to see the cultural influences that had been shaping me and provided me with the key to exploring all the issues I face as the DoEA in British society and the world. I now understood that for a DoEA the self is effectively separated from knowledge in the British education system as we continue to be inculturated into seeing the world through the eyes of the ethnic majority – our re-creators.

Studied and understood dynamically, history provides us with a record of our lives, behaviours and activities as a people – our glories, successes, failures, kindnesses and cruelties. Without delving into the past it is impossible to understand how the present came into being and what the trends are for the near future. An understanding of history provides focus and a sense of historical continuity and thus a vision for the future. People have attempted to highlight the importance of having an historical perspective of one's self and group in time and space: 'A people without history are like a tree without roots' argued Marcus Garvey (Campbell, 1999), the African descended philosopher and nationalist. 'For others a knowledge of the history of their people is a civic duty whilst for Jews it is a sacred duty' claimed Maurice Samuel (1963), highlighting the source of the strength of the Jews as a nation. Freire (1970) argues that for us to be active agents in shaping our own realities we need to have a socio-historical perspective on our position in society now. Black children schooled in Britain are not given this historical context. Consequently they lack self-knowledge because they are not nurtured and socialised to acquire it through knowing and understanding history from their own legitimate perspective. This supports the argument for bicultural socialisation put by DeAnda (1984).

History as mythology and legend

Understanding history as myth, legend and saga provided another lens for critically engaging with British history and how it might be presented. In '*The*

Falsification of the Afrikan Consciousness' Wilson (1993) provides insights into the intimate link between history, culture and personality. Exploring European history as mythology, as propaganda and as the creator of personality Wilson (1993) suggests that

> ... European history's principle function is to first separate us (as Africans) from the reality of ourselves and separate us from the reality of the world; to separate us from the reality of our history and to separate us from its ramifications.

Wilson (1993), a psychiatrist, suggests that mythology can be understood as a form of denial of reality:

> If a memory is too painful to be recalled, if recalling it means suffering, pain, shame, guilt and other negative things, the individual may not only deny the reality of that memory and experience but may actually create a mythology in their places. By becoming obsessed and caught up in that mythology, he uses it as a means of keeping out of his conscious memory the traumatic experiences that he fears.

The primary function of mythology is to maintain self-esteem thus ensuring that a people's self-esteem and vision of who they are is maintained through the projection of their history as mythology. This is true of British history and similar claims have been made for Afrocentricity, which works for the benefit of Africans. Afrocentricity (Asante, 1992), which places the African at the centre of its historical analysis and challenges European historiography, poses a threat to Europeans and the workings of their societies.

Mythology also maintains European power, domination and control: it has become part of our mental structure, a tool of intellection, comprehension, of dealing with and relating to the world. Wilson shows how European mythology organises the world and human behaviour, moulds character and motivates or demotivates. Mythology is important in determining the dominant discourse. This process and the repression of feminine consciousness, as argued by Eisler (1991), are striking in their similarities.

Wilson demonstrates clearly how history can also be used to intimidate and therefore destroy confidence and the capacity of individuals to think for themselves and to believe that they are capable of being creators. The impression of intimidation remains in our consciousness even when the overall content is lost. It becomes a dynamic source of behavioural orientation toward the world, lest there are black British people, including myself, who would claim defensively that they have no memory of British/European history anyway. While I can seldom recall the details of British and European history, I have been in no doubt about the 'might' and the 'right', of the UK. What Wilson shows is that history is not a casual thing that one picks up while passing through school. It becomes a part of one's total orientation toward the world. This insight raises questions about how slavery will be presented and taught as part of the school curriculum given the current unconscious bi-cultural competence of the majority of teachers in the education system.

Many of the DoEAs choose to repress awareness of their history, afraid to confront it because of the anxiety, anger, fear, guilt and shame we feel when we read or watch some aspects of the African experience we would rather not identify or be identified with. The existence of the race taboo compounded by white silence, also results in non-engagement with the issues by the DoEAs. We think and perhaps hope that we have escaped the effects by this avoidance. The few individuals or groups who articulate these issues are typically identified as extremists, fanatics and troublemakers (Pryce, 1979). Wilson (1993:34) reminds us that

> ... exactly because the past is forgotten, it rules unchallenged. To be transcended it must first be remembered. Social amnesia is society's repression of remembrance.

This social amnesia and the confusion and despair it can lead to, as in my own case, were discussed in the previous chapter. Wilson further reminds us.

> ... But we should heed the fact that a person and people who suffer from social amnesia live lives that are determined by fear, anxiety, terror and trauma. When we attempt to escape our history because we're afraid of it, when we escape know-ledge because it terrifies and makes us feel ashamed, then it is terror and fear and shame that determines our lives. We then live, not in terms of our reality and in terms of the integration of our reality but in terms of what we are afraid of, i.e. what we are ashamed of, what we are trying to hide, what we are trying not to confront ourselves with. Life is then lived in terms of denial, in terms of escape and addiction.

This chapter has provided a much needed backdrop to the life and organisa-tional experiences shared in the previous chapters which make the black ex-periences that lead to psychic disorientation, confusion and despair easily understood. A 500-year relationship between the DoEAs and DoSOs and not just 50 years has been unearthed and surfaced. The need to maintain a wall of silence between the two groups, critical to this relationship, is seen in the working of the race taboo. This silence has been shown to work to maintain the DoEAs in a subordinated place relative to the DoSOs. Unconsciousness based on a lack of self-knowledge is helped by the DoSOs being responsible for the education of the DoEAs. Initially understanding this history fuelled a sense of hopelessness as I contemplated the entrenched nature of my posi-tion as the DoEAs relative to that of the DoSOs. The evidence suggests that to date the DoEAs have not been successful in breaking out of the master-slave relationship created during slavery because of our sustained unconscious-ness.

The on-going intra-psychic outcomes of the creation of the black-white duality – an oppositional and yet symbiotic relationship which pits whites against blacks and blacks against whites – is more important than the facts of history. As the DoEAs we have been kept away from our ethnic roots and yet not embraced by the group who took us away. Instead we have been trapped in a cultural limbo leading to insecurity, confusion, despair and hopelessness.

Generative educators

For us as educators, the research underpinning these early chapters challenges our fitness for the purpose of preparing our young for effective lives if we are ignorant or in denial about the knowledge and perspective shared here. This needs to be studied by both the DoEAs and the DoSOs if we are to combine our efforts to educate a new generation.

The DoEAs have seen culture operating as process as opposed to something which is fixed that was taken away from us. It is in the choices we make on a moment by moment basis that the culture we are evolving is based. Our dysfunctional adaptation to a culture of inferiorisation, poverty and deprivation, silence, fear, avoidance, anger, aggression, and reactiveness is the culture that we are unwittingly passing on to our children. We accuse the ethnic majority of egocentric domination but fail to recognise our own egocentric submissiveness (Elder and Paul, 2004). Because of our ignorance and lack of courage the experience of the DoEAs in British society relative to the white ethnic majority has been largely trivialised and undermined. Our children continue to be unconsciously assimilated into black British culture under the control of the white British culture of the ethnic majority. We need to follow the example of the Jews in making the teaching of our history a sacred duty. In knowing and teaching our own children their history we place responsibility on teachers in the school system to be accountable where this history and the education of our children are concerned. We also afford our children centricity by ensuring that they are biculturally socialised. In this way we will be able to hold the school system accountable. However, fear, shame and long-term internalised oppression prevent us from engaging with this history which keeps us locked into this ongoing dysfunctional cycle. We need courage. And this courage can be incrementally developed through understanding what it means to be whole human beings and developing conscious bicultural competence as a life strategy.

5

The five dimensional human being: working with visible and invisible legacies

People travel to wonder at the height of mountains, at the huge waves of the sea, at the long courses of rivers, at the vast compass of the ocean, at the circular motion of the stars; and they pass by themselves without wondering.
(St Augustine 399 AD)

The specific form that pseudo speciation takes is the creation of *negative identities* ... what makes these identity materials negative is that they are proffered by the dominant cultural group with a patronising, even condemnatory attitude. The transaction serves to prop up the chauvinism of the master group. Sadly, its victims occasionally yield to the force of convention and accept the roles proffered so as to survive in a hostile environment. (Hoover *et al*, 1997)

... freedom begins in the mind – the freedom to know, to think, is basic to all other freedoms. To enslave a man's mind, to keep knowledge from him, to manipulate his processes of thinking, is a graver sin against him than to restrict his physical freedom. For it is with the mind, as well as the heart, that a man reaches up to God and out to his fellow men. The freedom to know is vital, because our choices are what determine our destiny, 'and the choice we can never make is the choice we have never heard of'. (Anderson, 1977)

Introduction

Developing conscious bicultural competence demands that we work with the visible and invisible legacies bequeathed to us by history and our ancestors. We must know what it means for us to be whole human beings if we are to make successful life-enhancing interventions. Hence the necessity of distinguishing between what it means to be human as opposed to black or white. Learning that I had been culturally determined beyond my conscious awareness demanded that I should now understand how this process worked. The common view that I returned to where I came from (ie Africa) was unrealistic and did not resonate with me. In this chapter the five-dimensional human being model which has been developed as integral to self-understanding is introduced. Culture is defined and its function in human life is explored, showing it to be the integrative force vital to human existence which if not given attention can have devastating effects on human life. This generic model is contrasted with the model of the human being who has been dehumanised but is largely unaware of it. The consequences for ethnic culture are considered. There has not been any significant research into the impact of slavery on the psychological, emotional and spiritual well-being of the DoEAs. The same is also true for the DoSOs. This silence is the result of black socialisation. The implications of this research are significant for understanding the mental health issues faced by DoEAs in British society. The cost of silence for the human status of not just the DoEAs, but the human race as a whole is also considered.

The previous chapters showed how black culture is an externally imposed cultural disorder placed over the DoEAs which has now taken on a life of its own (McWhorter, 2001). This chapter considers the human being to whom culture is so critical and then the nature of culture itself.

Educators as cultural practitioners

Many of us as educators and parents are normalised to identifying or being identified as white or black whereas being human is taken for granted. Robb (1997) suggests:

> ... all educators, whether they are aware of it or not, are striving to be authentic educators. Authentic educators attempt to alleviate both symptomatic and fundamental (ontic), human needs. Humanness is found to be fundamental (ontic) needs plus the actions necessary to alleviate them, and the author finds education to be synonymous with helping educands identify and alleviate fundamental (ontic) need. Unless educators know what fundamental human needs are and what is required to alleviate them, the quality of their educative teaching is limited and they cannot claim to be doing the best possible for their educands. Consequently, a study of humanness should be included in the curriculum for educators of adults.

Considered in the context of the findings so far Robb's idea suggests that government, including the Teacher Development Agency (TDA), needs to take this area of study into account right across the education system if they are sincere in providing education for one nation (1990 Trust) where the human needs of all members of the society can be met. What are the consequences for the DoEAs and DoSOs of being automatically socialised into differential cultures in British society in a way which is beyond our conscious level of awareness? All teachers, DoEAs and DoSOs, who have been socialised into British culture will have developed the double consciousness inherent in the existence of two subcultures. Where this double consciousness is not recognised and worked through educators will automatically transmit a cultural dysfunction.

My autobiographical research reveals the fact that the majority of the DoSOs who were responsible for providing me with an education were not ethically entitled to do so. Without an awareness of the extent to which their own humanity has been distorted by white and black cultures and how their group consciousness conditions them to see DoEAs as inferior to themselves, they should not be socialising members of this group. They can only be socialising us into an inferior black culture relative to their own white superior culture, wittingly and unwittingly. It is essential for such teachers to get back in touch with their own humanity before they attempt to educate other people's children and future generations. As educators we must recognise ourselves as cultural practitioners involved in the teaching and learning process of cultural socialisation. Otherwise we are unconsciously engaged at the first three levels of Kotre's (1983) typology whereas as educators we have a responsibility to be consciously engaged at the fourth level of culture.

Human needs

Figure 5.1 depicts four dimensions basic to all human beings: mind, emotions and spirit/consciousness, all carried in the fourth dimension – the physical body.

Figure 5.1: The human make-up

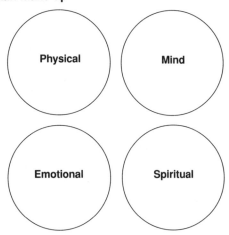

To succeed in life the four dimensions of the human being must be understood and integrated into an interdependent whole.

The physical body can be understood as the container for the other dimensions, giving them visibility through self-expression in the physical world. The physical body acknowledges our ethnicity and therefore the group to which we belong and with whom we have mutual responsibility. The physical body also defines our gender. While our physical bodies are not the be all and end all of who we are, as I had been socialised to think as the DoEAs, they differentiate us from others through distinctive features and qualities.

The qualities of the unique soul seeking self-expression is hidden within the complexity of the human being and revealed through the self-consciousness of the individual in the spiritual dimension. Other concepts typically used to describe this spiritual dimension are intuition, inner teacher and consciousness. This dimension can be understood as the genie in Aladdin's lamp. It is the source of the human being and the other dimensions can be understood as tools for the self-expression of the inner self. Chile and Simpson (2004) define this spiritual dimension as the interconnecting force of oneness dwelling within every culture and every geographical community. As people search for meaning, spirituality becomes embedded in their ways of life informing their ethics and their desires.

The *mind dimension* is the main centre through which information from a variety of sources, internal and external, is passed through the human being. The mind needs to be educated and trained to develop its faculties and, importantly, to understand how it works. Whether true or false, beliefs accepted in the mind dimension and internalised as truth becomes manifest in the life of the individual. It is when the individual is controlled by external sources such as the authority of culture externally imposed, that this dimension dominates and the spiritual dimension forced to take a backseat.

The *emotions dimension* is the centre of feeling, the source of the senses enabling us to experience the world and enjoy a range of emotions. The emotions are a source of energy for achieving our goals and contributing to the whole being.

Thus we consist of mind, body, feelings and spirit. These dimensions of the self are interdependent with the key being the spirit. It is Frankl's (1984) view that the spiritual core, and only the spiritual core, warrants and constitutes oneness and wholeness enabling us to exercise our urge for meaning, to envisage our goals and to move beyond our instinctual needs, to achieve self-transcendence.

The integrative role of culture

The means by which these four dimensions are integrated is shown in the central rectangle of Figure 5.2

Figure 5.2: The five dimensional human being

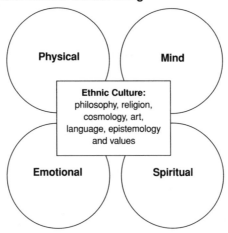

We see here that the fifth dimension, culture, is the *human task*, the purpose of life, which we as humans work out for ourselves. Culture is the authentic creative strivings of the individuals and a people growing out of their day-by-day engagement with the world as they seek to make life-enhancing choices that enable their group to continue. Kotre (1983) says the quality of a culture can be assessed by the extent to which it facilitates its young to thrive.

For authentic cultural development the spiritual dimension of the individual and group must be protected, nurtured and honoured because it is the inner invisible life giving the individual their human dignity and integrity and contributes to group culture. The Ancients believed that all ethnic groups, through their culture, have a specific contribution to make to the whole. This is because the universal awareness of being expresses itself differentially through each group that makes up the human race (Gorringe, 2004). For a group, or individual, to attain its specific destiny as part of this greater plan, it has a responsibility to live from its own self-consciousness, developing a culture which is derived from the self-consciousness of its membership. The culture so derived is kept in various ways in the constituent parts that make up culture. The rectangle in Figure 5.2 includes philosophy, cosmology, metaphysics, religion and art. This culture is systematically transmitted down the generational chain to remind each new generation of their reason for being and the contribution they have to make to the whole. Miller and Yudice (2002:2) define culture thus:

> Culture gives man (sic) the ability to reflect upon himself. It is through culture that man expresses himself, becomes aware of himself, recognises his incompleteness, questions his own achievements, seeks untiringly for new meanings and creates works through which he transcends his limitations.

Culture is the product of ethnic identification. It is group specific and has nothing at all to do with skin colour.

Ethnicity, culture and the human being

Smith (1991) defines an ethnic group as:

> ... a reference group called upon by people who share a common history and culture, who may be identifiable because they share similar physical features and values and who, through the process of interacting with each other and establishing boundaries with others, identify themselves as being a member of that group. Ethnic identity is the sum total of group members' feelings about those values, symbols and common histories that identify them as a distinct group ... A person does not belong to an ethnic group by choice, rather, he or she must be born into such a group and becomes related to it through emotional and symbolic ties.

Ethnic groups are part of the master plan to take care of the world: the creation of black and white cultures is a perversion of this plan. Ethnic groups are responsible for taking care of their membership by creating culture and establishing structures, systems and processes to facilitate their members on their journey through life. Those who have been unconsciously assimilated into black British culture will be largely unaware of this.

Education is the process whereby culture is transmitted to new generations of the group so that they can build on the knowledge and understanding transmitted instead of starting from scratch. Thus each generation benefits from those who have gone before as well as having legacies to create for generations to come. Culture can either be a beacon of light revealing to us what it means to be a human being and how best to live our lives, as understood by our ancestors, or a veil, an externally imposed cultural disorder, blinding us to the reality of what it means to be human, as in the case of the DoEAs.

The dehumanisation of enslaved Africans

Having interrogated black culture and engaged with my historical journey and experiences it is now easier to understand my experiences in the world today and what I need to do to work with the visible and invisible legacies of slavery, colonisation and neo-colonisation discussed in chapter four. As I consider what it means to be human Figure 5.3 suggests what the outcomes of slavery are likely to be for the DoEAs.

Figure 5.3: The black five dimensional dehumaniser doer

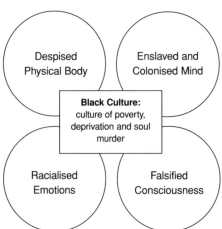

The consequences of an externally imposed cultural disorder is seen in Figure 5.3 in a design for living that was brutally and inhumanely imposed in terms of its impact on the four dimensions of the human being. Enslaved Africans learned to despise their own physiognomy as they internalised white perceptions of what it meant for them to be African. The force with which this design for living was imposed meant that their self-consciousness was repressed and eventually falsified as white consciousness was forced on them. Their emotions became racialised as they were forced to repress any signs of feelings in front of their white masters. Martinas (1992) defines racialised emotions as the creation and recreation of 'carefully manipulated racialised emotions in peoples of colour and in white people ... produces emotions of suppressed and explosive rage ... On a daily basis, suppressed rage can be deadly to one's mental and physical health ...'. But, black people are not the only group to suffer from racialised emotions. In this way enslaved Africans were thus transformed from human beings into dehumanised doers. This was the beginning of the oppositional relationship that developed between blacks and whites.

This dehumanising experience has never been reversed. After hundreds of years in slavery the DoEAs walked out of chattel slavery and into colonisation and neo-colonisation. This experience has evolved into what we know today as 'black culture'. This has evolved in many ways from what it was during chattel slavery because of the creative strivings of the DoEAs as we have sought to make do with what we have. Black culture has not been interrogated for inherent dysfunctions so that they can be eradicated from the life experience of the DoEAs. The major dysfunction of black culture is that it is the creation of Europeans, one of two sub-cultures embedded in British culture to manage the diversity of the empire putting in place power differentials between the two groups. The visible and invisible legacies of this experience continue to be transmitted down the generational chain of the DoEAs. They also continue to be externally administered by the DoSOs and result in racism. Given that these two cultures have transcended the passage of time it becomes clear why and how Africans and the DoEAs remain in an inferiorised space as well as why slavery still exists in the 21st century.

Figure 5.3 makes it clear that black culture, the culture into which I have been born, has not been specifically developed with my best interests in mind. It is not a valued culture so it has not been codified and is not consciously trans-mitted as a means of preserving valued ways of being. Instead, unconscious socialisation into black culture results in non-generative outcomes for its members. By imposing on me the black identity, the English effectively dis-placed internal processes of maturation and growth by substituting identity foreclosure as shown in the previous chapters. In contrast to Miller and Yudice's (2002) definition of culture black culture and identity provides me with nothing to reflect on and aspire to. In addition the race taboo and white silences around it cause the anxieties, doubts and fears I have around these issues to remain shut down inside of me causing havoc to my human make-up. This is the first opportunity I have had to engage with this experience and how it still continues to impact on me today. I have carried out this research in opposition to strong cultural forces. What does this experience suggest about the human status of the DoSOs?

The dehumanisation of slave-owners

When figure 5.4 opposite is juxtaposed against Figure 5.3 it reveals the out-comes of slavery for the two groups. The being outcomes for the DoSOs as compared to the doing outcomes for the DoEAs should not be missed.

A perversion was created in the thinking of slave owners/Europeans in that they positioned themselves as being superior relative to Africans to satisfy their desire for wealth and world domination. This perversion has been perpetuated over hundreds of years during which Europeans have been born into white culture in relation to black culture. The sub-speciation necessary for instilling into the minds of human beings the existence of different races as opposed to one human race distinguished by different ethnic families became a standard way of thinking. White consciousness through the growth of the empire became a standard way of thinking which was imposed on other groups. Nell Painter (1995) has written in some depth about the costs of slavery for both groups.

Figure 5.4: The white five dimensional dehumanised being

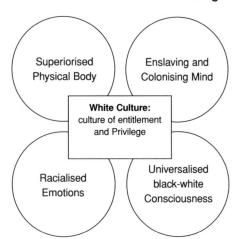

The costs of dehumanisation in multicultural and post-colonial societies

In multicultural post-colonial societies, cross-cultural and cross-racial understanding and misunderstanding involve all of us in our emotional and mental dimensions. Understanding of this is neglected in our education to our detriment. For many years education in the UK has excluded consideration of the emotions and spirit and has focused only the mind and physical body as determinants of individual and group abilities. These subjects have come onto the agenda of some business schools only in the last decade. Consequently, the deeper inner life occurring unconsciously which consciously developed culture is meant to support has been neglected to the society's detriment. In the previous chapter we looked at the silenced conflicts between Africa, Britain and the Caribbean which have been internalised. Timimi (1996) describes the situation well:

> For whites (meaning those identified with being white, as well as those parts of the self identified with being white), despised aspects of the self can be projectively identified in blacks. Awareness of the projection of these despised aspects of the self is not needed by virtue of the position of privilege given to the white object. Franz Fanon (1967) described this lack of awareness amongst whites as a devastating pathology at the heart of western culture, a pathology based on a denial of difference. Whites did not need to know about these phenomena as the psychological trauma of discrimination did not affect them. Blacks (meaning those identified with being black, as well as those parts of the self identified with being black), as recipients of these projections, are, in effect, being asked to act as containers for these hated parts of the self. Here a whole range of experiences from language and culture through to a belief in one's ability can be undermined if it is experienced as being black. In this scheme, reciprocal projective identifications

locate the desirable aspects of the self in whites. Such dynamics will occur not only in the landscape of multi-racial cities but also within the internal landscape of the mind, with whites and blacks separated with paranoid anxieties suffusing the scene when one tries to become integrated with the other.

This means of relating is extended to other ethnic groups, resulting in Feagin's (2000) conceptualisation of the white to black status continuum. The defining cost of the dehumanisation being discussed is the silence that has built up around it. Silence is costly to the human being because it inhibits self-expression which is the whole purpose of life. Knowing that behind the silence is something that is deeply wrong is deeply wounding to the human spirit. No wonder Holdt (1997) observes that whites don't like the blacks they live with or the ones they have hurt because they have to buy into silence in a self-protective stance which inhibits their own self-expression.

For this and many more reasons understanding what it means to be human and understanding the inner landscape of the mind, emotions and spirit is essential to effective conscious bicultural competence. We learn that neither the black nor white experience is normal or healthy. What is clear is that the body and its skin-colour have been used by Caucasians to shape beliefs, thoughts and behaviours about what it means to be human, undermining the critical dimensions of the spirit and emotions. This has been to the detriment of the human race. Only when we understand the significance and integrity of culture to the human being can we fully understand the importance of being consciously biculturally competent. This is especially important because of the extent of migration amongst groups in a globalising world. The significance placed on biculturalism in this book is related to British culture because of the consequence of colonisation and the empire.

Creating a re-humanised British culture

One of the most encouraging and hopeful statements I have come across during my research is the idea that culture is process and therefore incomplete. Figure 5.5 opposite considers human attributes from the perspective of the whole human to show how the human attributes of both blacks and whites have been distorted which allows us to see how we can transform the experience.

The transformation of British culture into a culture for whole human beings will effectively dismantle the current dysfunctional nature of British culture. Figure 5.6 opposite reveals the inner culture which is being achieved as I worked with the insights gained through this research to bring about the desired change.

Figure 5.5 Comparison of the Whole Human with 'Whites' and 'Blacks'

Attributes	Whole Human	White	Black
Physical	Unique	Superiorised	Inferiorised
Mental	Creative	Enslaving/greedy	Enslaved/colonised
Emotional	Power source	Racialised	Racialised
Spiritual	Original	Falsified/ego	Falsified/slave
Individual soulprint	Unique	Expressed	Repressed
Ethnic soulprint	Unique culture	Privileged	Deprivation
Ethnic family	Unique	Caucasian	Negroid (African)
History	Unique	Universalised	Repressed/denied
Current context	Global	Global	Closed systems
Philosophy	Spiritual	Ownership	Struggle/poverty

Figure 5.6: The rehumanised British African-Caribbean

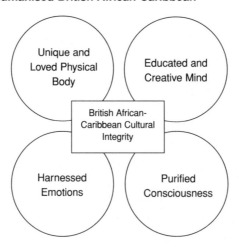

The re-humanised British African-Caribbean (BAC) perspective is based on a new psychological contract with myself, knowledge (historical, ethnic, cultural, emotional, spiritual, mental/psychological) and being an autodidactic learner. BAC cultural integrity is thus protected as the means by which the well-being of the individual and group is ensured. The dysfunctions of black culture have been replaced by the benefits of a culture which is designed with the interests of BACs at its core. Bicultural socialisation is a fundamental feature of BAC culture, facilitating ethnic identity development as an important life-task. The extent to which the need for cultural integrity for the

DoEAs is understood and met is the extent to which effective and conscious bicultural competence can be assumed to have been achieved.

In a similar way a re-humanised English perspective would look something like Figure 5.7

Figure 5.7: The re-humanised British-English

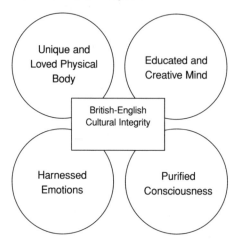

To be able to work effectively with British culture in the ways suggested here we need to understand the nature of culture.

Understanding the nature of culture

Subordinated to whites for hundreds of years, the DoEAs have not had the opportunity to be responsible for ourselves and to take on leadership responsibilities for ourselves as a group. Instead, we have been slotted into a society created for another group at a peripheral service role position which has been predetermined for us by that group. DoEAs have generally accepted the leadership of whites as natural as it as continued post-slavery. What then does my existential crisis of meaning mean for the on-going black experience? The clear message is that the neo-colonial model under which I have been socialised and which operates so restrictively on my life chances is no longer appropriate to my aspirations. I had believed and internalised ideas of equality of opportunity and meritocracy before realising they were only rhetoric in the mind-world of many DoSOs. So, how long can Britain continue the old psychological contract with the descendants of her former slaves? I have evolved and have developed conscious bicultural competence. Only now, understanding what it means to be a whole human being, and having negotiated a new psychological contract with myself, can I consciously think about how it is appropriate for me, as the DoEAs, to live relative to the DoSOs and other ethnic groups in the 21st century.

Nobles (1985) has captured the dynamism of culture as 'a process which gives people a general design for living and patterns for interpreting their reality'. The knowledge developed here makes an important contribution to a general design which can be used in developing a more functional British African-Caribbean and British-English culture. Hofstede's (1980) view of culture as software is important.

> Every nation has a considerable moral investment in its own dominant mental software, which amply explains the common hesitation to make cultural differences discussable.

The DoEAs have been incorporated into black British culture through unconscious assimilation, unaware of the existence of two subcultures. We need to think about the vested interests DoSOs might have in maintaining the ongoing relationship between the two groups under British culture. The DoSOs are unlikely to do so this because it would highlight national vested interests, which nations prefer to downplay and act on rather than discuss and analyse. Nevertheless, the mental programming or software of the mind that holds blacks and whites together in British culture is that of white supremacy and black inferiority. This software ensures that each group keeps to the domain of British culture prescribed for them. Do we, as DoEAs and DoSOs want to stay in this position now that we are aware of how it has been created and maintained?

Bowles (1990) throws further light on the role society, and hence the family, plays in this process.

> What the individual chooses to deny about him/herself will be dictated by the society, which will define normative standards of thought and action ... together with unique features that stem from the particular form of socialisation.

I gained further insight from the idea of culture as

> an open-ended creative dialogue of sub-cultures, of insiders and outsiders, of diverse factions ... Culture is not simply a static field, providing opportunities and constraints for a movement; it is a contested terrain.' (Fantasia and Hirsch 1995; 145)

This suggests that culture is a social process involving a range of different interest groups, insiders and outsiders, and that it is inherently flexible and adaptable, with the ability to sustain differing sub-cultures within its overall structure as seen in black and white cultures. That idea that the DoEAs co-exist in multicultural Britain would demonstrate the inherent adaptability and flexibility of British culture if this were the case. The truth is nearer the view that the DoEAs have been incorporated into a post-colonial society relative to the DoSOs. In either case, what many DoEAs do not realise is how we are unwittingly co-creators of British culture and are actively involved in shaping, maintaining and perpetuating its dysfunctions. Culture as process is achieved through the daily choices we make so we are all actively involved in reproducing culture as process, both consciously and unconsciously, though we might not like to take responsibility for this.

Ani (1994) suggests the flexibility and adaptability of culture when she states

> culture is tenacious, ingeniously using varied techniques to ensure its own survival. (p61)

This emphasises the political nature of culture: individuals and groups are always acting to protect their own interests. As one person moves to bring about change someone else is likely to make a countermove to ensure the *status quo* is maintained. Conscious awareness is vital so that countermoves can be anticipated and responded to appropriately.

The functions of culture

Connerley and Pederson (2005) draw on others to identify culture:

> [It is] ... the source of ties that bind members of societies through an elusive 'socially constructed constellation consisting of such things as practices, competencies, ideas, schemas, symbols, values, norms, institutions, goals, constitutive rules, artefacts, and modifications of the physical environment' (Fiske, 2002, p.85). These internalized rules create traditions that often go deeper than reason (Stuart, 2004).'

Blacks and whites it seems are unconsciously bound together in British society by rules of which many of us, especially as DoEAs, are largely unaware. Mazrui (1990) and Ani (1994) have highlighted fundamental functions that culture serves in human society and world politics as follows

- It is a lens of perception and cognition – worldview, axiology, epistemology, ontology and systems of logic

- It 'tells' its members 'what to do' thus creating a voice of prescriptive authority providing motives for human behaviour. What makes a person respond behaviourally in a particular manner is arguably partly cultural in origin

- It is criteria of evaluation, and the creation of shared symbols and meanings. What is deemed better or worse, ugly or beautiful, moral or immoral, attractive or repulsive, is partly a child of culture

- It is a basis of individual and group identity and thus creates a sense of collective cultural identity

- It is a differentiation aspect in that it stratifies its members
- It is a mode of communication and therefore understanding

Generative education

How can we be effective educators without the knowledge contained in this chapter? Surely this knowledge must be central to the teaching and learning process in our classrooms. Educational philosophers over the centuries have left us this knowledge about what it means to be human and about how we ought to go about the task of educating our young (Palmer, 2001) but it seems not to be commonly applied in our schools and universities. We see that ethnic culture is crucial to well-being and yet DoEAs have been left without it as they have been unconsciously assimilated into British culture where they are also unconsciously socialised into black culture, the culture into which enslaved Africans were inducted during slavery. It is also evident that being taught by members of the ethnic majority further disadvantages members of this group, given the silencing of the history of ethnic conflict between these two groups. Here we gain important insights into why the deafening silence identified by Matsuura (2004) surrounds this experience.

The significance of this chapter for the DoEAs cannot be overstated. It contains the basis of the knowledge required for recreating ourselves and our lives. Our goal must be conscious bicultural competence as we challenge ourselves to live everyday as whole human beings. This requires us to pay attention to our own lives and to be attuned to all five dimensions of the self ensuring that they function as a harmonised whole. When the harmony breaks down or seems to be unachievable we know something is wrong and our task becomes to find a resolution. As the DoEAs we have been living without harmony as a natural outcome of life in Britain as we have internalised the oppositional black-white duality.

The DoSOs also have similar work to do. They must challenge themselves about their fitness for teaching other peoples children, especially the DoEAs, when they are unconscious of the dysfunctions of the culture they are transmitting on a daily basis. The five hundred year-old relationship between the DoEAs and the DoSOs means that we have learned to live within the constraints of a dysfunctional relationship which has been normalised – hence the need for silence and unconsciousness.

Informal educators in the home must now work with formal educators in the education system to achieve outcomes appropriate to a democracy. The next chapter offers further insights into the role we have to play in re-humanising British culture through our role as educators.

6

British culture as a dehumanising project

Apart from the wounding of the souls of continents, colonialism also – paradoxically – achieved an accidental serendipity. It brought people together in a way that might not have happened for hundreds of years. For example, as a result of its over-reaching, Britain began by colonising half the world and now finds half the world in its territory, within its history, subtly altering its psyche. Things work both ways. (Okri, 1997:100)

To understand the manner in which culture contours the expression of human generativity we must examine specific cultures at a deep level. (St Aubin, 2004)

When an entire culture ceases to care about nurturing and protecting human life – as I believe ours has – we must examine the deeper meanings of caring and not caring, our individual capacities and failure to love our children and ourselves. (Swigart, 1991)

The racism that we know was born in Europe and America from the cultural need to justify doing to black people, doing to Africans, what would not morally or legally be done to white people, and least of all to Europeans. To justify the enslavement of Africans, in short, it was culturally necessary to believe that Africans were inherently and naturally less than human, were beings of a somehow subhuman, nonhuman, nature ... and its success in this dehumanising project needs no demonstration here, for it is obvious in our culture to this day. (Davidson, 1994:320)

Introduction

Having an enhanced understanding of my responsibilities as an educator, both as a parent and a lecturer in higher education, challenged me
not to continue to collude with the dysfunction inherent in Britain's
racialised culture. Earlier chapters have described the relationship of the
DoEAs to British culture. The focus of this chapter is on how this relationship
is maintained and perpetuated through social structures and processes,
especially when British culture is understood as an ethnic culture struggling
to work with the diversity it now finds on its shore. In the first section the
positioning of the DoEAs relative to the ethnic majority and to other ethnic
minority groups is considered. In the second section the institution of social
interaction is introduced as the means by which old slavery has taken on new
forms.

The politics of positionality

Portrayed diagrammatically the DoEAs, as a collective, operate at the margins
of British society in a state of unconscious bicultural competence/ incompetence as seen here:

Figure 6.1: Relationship between Black and White Cultures within British Culture

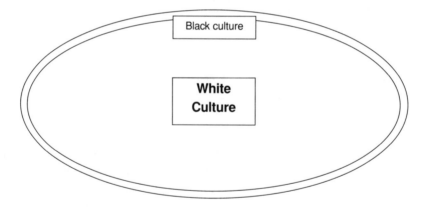

In Figure 1.1, where the bicultural matrix was first introduced, there is an
implicit assumption that reference is being made to two distinct national cultures about which awareness needs to be maintained. However, as my understanding evolved it became apparent that British culture consists of two subcultures: black cultures and white. This idea is represented in Figure 6.1 where
England consists of a white predominantly English culture with the DoEAs
occupying positions at the margins of the society, as an underclass. This marginal position is where we have been co-opted for the secondary labour

market which serves the needs of the DoSOs. The same is likely to be true for the DoEAs in any white majority society such as Scotland, Ireland or the US and is currently a fixed arrangement. It confirms the idea of a neo-colonial relationship for the DoEAs relative to the DoSOs but is hidden behind the idea of a multicultural society. To think of Britain as a post-colonial society is to see our location more clearly. The English – the DoSOs – are seen to occupy a position of centricity and are privileged by white culture whereas the DoEAs are decentred in terms of our ethnic roots. We exist, therefore, as on-lookers and even captives of white English culture, a culture that we cannot be a part of because we are excluded on the basis of our skin-colour and our ante-cedents (ONS, 2003). It is not our ethnic folk culture (Gorringe, 2004) of origin. And yet it contains us in a cultural limbo.

The situation of the DoEAs amounts to a politics of positionality based on the assumption that no group is in and of itself oppressed or marginal – but only in relation to something else. DoEAs have been socially constructed to be op-pressed and marginal in relation to the DoSOs. Consequently, authentic English folk culture is daily undermined, to the chagrin and loss of many English, going unacknowledged overtly in favour of British culture which is encoded with black and white cultures. British culture manages the diversity which the empire brought about and which English culture is not equipped to do. Many of us are unconsciously aware of these facts as we go about our daily lives in Britain: this is unconscious bicultural competence.

Figure 6.1 suggests, however, that the DoSOs are not locked into white culture in the same damaging way that the DoEAs are locked into black culture. Living within the boundaries of their authentic ethnic folk cultures they are able to provide differential ethnic socialisation for their children dependent on their culture of origin (i.e. English, Scottish, Irish and Welsh). Their his-tories have not been repressed nor their experiences silenced. This idea is evident in books like *Watching the English* (Fox, 2005) or Jeremy Paxman's (1999) book on the same subject. Whatever their ethnic group all Caucasians expect and receive the privilege of white culture which is an outcome of the institution of slavery. So it may well be that blacks and whites play out their prolonged and most significant battles in the psychic world of the DoEAs as noted by Timimi (1996) in the previous chapter. Thus ethnic identity has less to do with an ethnic group's culture *per se* than with the process by which groups defend the boundary that defines their culture when they are con-fronted with outsiders (Barth, 1969).

Multicultural or post-colonial Britain in the 21st century

In multicultural Britain each ethnic group is assumed to engage in the task of taking care of the interests of its membership. When the DoEAs are inappropriately acknowledged both as a community in its own right and an ethnic group with a culture of its own creation it is assumed this group is in a position to take care of the needs of its membership. If this doesn't happen it becomes a failure of the group. If we study the historical relationship between the DoEAs and the DoSOs more deeply we recognise why only the DoEAs as a group have been permanently subordinated, even in our ability to help ourselves. Figure 6.2 provides important insights into understanding the black position relative to whites in comparison to other ethnic groups who live in Britain.

Figure 6.2: How Britain Manages its Diversity

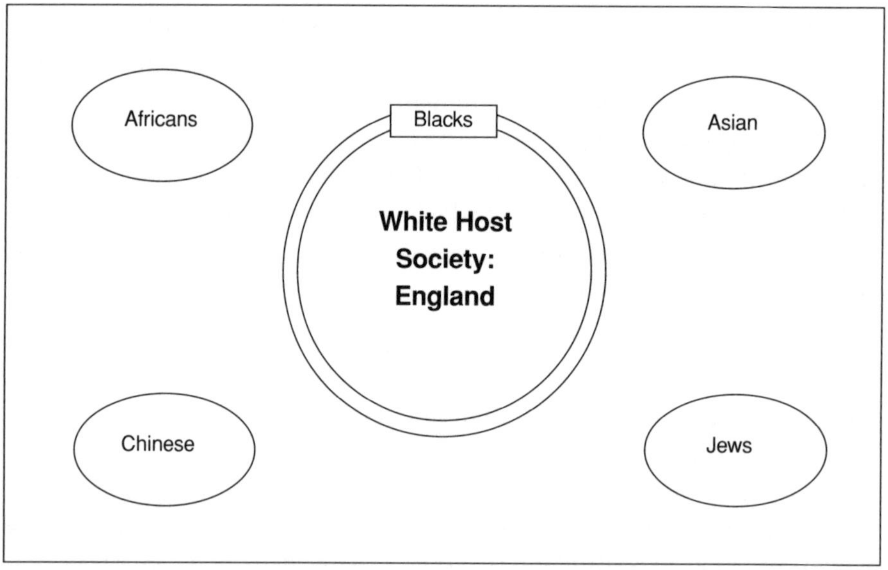

The common assumption that blacks hold a normalised position at the periphery of the society because of biological and genetic reasons becomes questionable in the context of this positioning. Figure 6.2 shows the position of the DoEAs relative to other ethnic groups, suggesting the historical reasons why we have remained in an inferior position relative not only to the DoSOs but to other ethnic groups. Black culture is seen to be an integral component of British culture situated within the boundaries of English culture, albeit at the periphery of the society, unlike other ethnic groups. At the periphery we do not and cannot form a cohesive community but operate as a social category (Banton, 1997). Britain thus continues, wittingly and unwittingly, to practice segregation between the DoEAs and the DoSOs through the invisible medium of black and white cultures. We are already aware that the DoSOs are key players administering black socialisation into black culture. From this depiction it is possible to see why the DoEAs are said to be the most 'integrated' of the minority groups in Britain (Madood, 2002). It also becomes evident why we are referred to as 'black' – relative to whites – and not as an ethnic minority group as seen in the label 'black and minority ethnic'. Figure 6.2 shows Britain to be managing through communities in the same way as governments across the western world (Phillips and Berman, 2003) in relation to ethnic communities whereas it is 'responsible' for the DoEAs in ways it is not responsible for other ethnic groupings.

Authentic ethnic groupings are seen to maintain their own ethnic cultural boundaries and therefore their integrity and are recognised as smaller ethnic groups operating within a diverse and plural society. In this sense they operate in a multicultural society. For example the Muslim community protects its cultural boundaries by negotiating with the government to protect their interests as a distinctive group. Smith (1976) observes that the attitude and orientation of Asians to the ethnic majority is different to that of the DoEAs. This difference is related to living in their own communities and having little to do with the ethnic majority.

The DoEAs continue to be governed by our white masters of previous eras. Members of the group continue to be unaware of this because of repeated references to the existence of a black community as well as to community leaders when these do not exist. Individuals acknowledged as community leaders by the establishment tend to be chosen by them and do not come from the grassroots of the group. Using Phillips and Berman's (2003) social quality measure confirms that the DoEAs do not function as a community. As a social category there are limited community resources or infrastructures to support the needs of its membership who are consequently left dependent on DoSOs. In chapter two I suggested that there are two levels of black culture: the victim culture administered by white culture and the creative strivings of the DoEAs as we strive to create a life-enhancing culture for ourselves. We must now turn to this latter culture in order to surface it and create a new ethnic identity for ourselves as a means of moving ourselves out of our current position in Britain.

New Slavery

It seems that our failures as the DoEAs to make sure that we understand how slavery works in order to ensure that it is not repeated is a contributing factor why the new forms of slavery we are witnessing in the world today is occurring. In understanding how the old slavery works today in the 21st century we need to study culture as process. This will help us understand how old forms of slavery have evolved into the new forms with which we live today. One of the key ways of freeing ourselves is to understand the agent of enslavement: in this case, British culture and its two subcultures. This is a major stumbling block for many DoEAs in British society who have immense problems in acknowledging the British dimension of our cultural socialisation. This is because of the role Britain has played in our subjugation as a group. This denial is indicative of the emotional turmoil and battle occurring in our inner cultural experience. Because our emotional turmoil largely goes unacknowledged we focus blame and resentment on the DoSOs. The challenge presented by history is to work through the anti-African, anti-black and anti-British values we have internalised within our own psychological world.

Culture as Social Process and Interaction

Understanding society as an invisible force, in that whilst we cannot see society we can experience how it acts on us through culture as process, is an important insight. Society understood as a force acts on both the DoEAs and the DoSOs through the invisible workings of the race taboo. As a result of the strength of the race taboo the individual who is the DoEAs has to be willing to face and endure the emotional labour which is inherent in staying with race as an issue in opposition to the working of the taboo. When we start to think about society as some sort of force, rather than as a physical entity, the focus of attention is moved onto how human behaviour is socially organised in terms of the social relationships people create and recognise over time (relationships that are given labels such as 'father', 'mother', 'blacks', 'whites' for example). To approach the concept of society from an angle that stresses the significance of social interaction as the key to understanding how society acts as a force upon people's behaviour provides us with important insights.

Talk-in-interaction

Heritage (2001) cites Schegloff (1992) as stating that 'talk-in-interaction' is 'the primordial site of human sociality'. This is because it is the fundamental resource through which the business of all societies is managed, their cultures transmitted, the identities of their participants affirmed and their social structures reproduced. Talk-in-interaction becomes recognisable as culture as process. I have engaged with this 'talk-in-interaction' in the institution in order to understand my actual relationship to whites as a black woman compared with the rhetoric which is espoused but not experienced.

Heritage argues that our ability to grasp the nature of the social world and to participate in it is dependent on our capacity, skill and resourcefulness as social interactants. This is dependent on the quality of our socialisation. White silence, the race taboo and a black culture of deprivation works against quality socialisation for blacks. From the outset it becomes apparent that my ability to function in the social world of white culture is effectively stymied by my positionality as a DoEA based on the racialisation of my identity. This is the significance of the difference between DoEAs and those who identify as Africans. DoEAs have a positionality as subordinated members of the English family in relation to whites as well as being the cultural 'other'. Rex (1982) comments on the unfairness of comparisons drawn between DoEAs and Asian given our differing backgrounds. My choosing to develop my understanding of the workings of the social world of blacks and whites as a DoEA made me threatening to the maintenance of the *status quo* and triggered the racialised emotions (Martinas, 1992) of both blacks and whites. In opting to use conversational analysis as a research tool I was able to gain important insights into interaction as a social institution as it occurs in everyday life.

The institution of social interaction/the interaction order

Heritage (2001) cites two key thinkers to make the interaction point: Goffman (1955, 1983) and Garfinkel (1967). Goffman theorises that social interaction is a form of social organisation in its own right which embodies a distinct moral and institutional order like other social institutions, such as the family, education and religion. Goffman termed this the interaction order comprising a complex set of interactional rights and obligations that are linked to 'face' (a person's immediate claims about who she is in an interaction) and more enduring features of personal identity. It becomes obvious that the 'face' of the DoEAs carries its own immediate message in the interaction order of English society, ie marginality and inferior status to whites. This status was enacted from the founding of slavery: the enslaved African was regarded as the legal inferior of the white man and denied all rights enjoyed by whites. Black evidence in a court of law was not acceptable against that of a white. The interaction order between blacks and whites which was established in slavery has continued through to modern day. It is also acknowledged by Troyna in chapter four to be embedded in white consciousness and transmitted intergenerationally.

Goffman further argued that the institutional interaction order has a particular social significance in that it underlies the operations of all the other institutions in society mediating the business they transact. The work of political, economic, educational, legal and other social institutions are all unavoidably transacted by means of the practices that make up the institution of social interaction. Goffman's (1967) central insight was that the institution of interaction has what he called a syntax. In the introduction to interaction ritual he observes, 'I assume that the proper study of interaction is not the individual and his psychology but rather the syntactical relations among the acts of different persons mutually present to one another'.

In the social institution of talk-in-action the syntactical relationship between blacks and whites is that black people are not ordinarily acknowledged by whites as being mutually present (refer to Figure 6.2). Goffman argues that the participants use this syntax, which is a socio-logic of interaction that provides for the sequential ordering of actions, to analyse one another's conduct and whether we are playing our roles as appropriate and determined by the culture. By looking at the choices people make within this syntax, judgements are made about personal motivations and identities. The colleague who described me as a 'uppity nigger' (see chapter two) was using this syntax in arriving at such a judgment based on my actions which were not about staying in the predetermined place allocated to me as a DoEA in British society.

This syntax, Goffman argued, is a core part of the moral order. It is the place where face (understood as the social value claimed in a given situation and role), self and identity are expressed and where they are also ratified, undermined or destroyed by the conduct of others. For example, teachers may decide that black boys are not being respectful enough, given the role expectations of the internalised and fixed black-white relationship, and so exclude them from the school system.

This idea can also be immediately related to the black organisational experience of invisibility, marginalisation and vulnerability detailed in chapter four (and by Alleyne (2004) in her paper). Here we see black professionals making the inauthentic choices necessary for survival but detrimental to the integrity of their human nature. The black employee who highlights the reality of their perceived marginalisation and invisibility is acknowledging their inferiorised status in the invisible social interaction order. They also show that they do not experience themselves as being mutually present to whites who do not perceive the necessity of engaging in the 'face work' necessary to suggest black social value. The vignettes in chapter three also provide excellent examples of this process.

I have studied the syntactical relationship between blacks and whites using deliberate and systematic second person action research/inquiry, whilst simultaneously engaging in first person action inquiry as a means of understanding the black/white relationship and how it is kept in place. Through longitudinal study of the range of different ethnic groups within the institutional context the differential relationship between whites and blacks and other ethnic groups revealed itself. This was before moving on to engage experientially with black-white relations (by making an unexpected move as a role-player – see Garfinkel below) to assess how flexible the boundaries of these assumptions are. I engaged in this behaviour towards the goal of transforming black/white relationships and outcomes within the institutional context. From my own findings these syntactical relations are the place where face, self and identity are expressed, ratified, undermined or destroyed by the conduct of DoSOs who are locked into the self-perception of being superior whites in relation to inferior blacks. I have also been able to witness how the force of British culture makes me respond according to a socially constructed pattern in ways I don't intend.

Shared methods of practical reasoning

Garfinkel (1967) argued that all human action and human institutions, including Goffman's (1967) interaction order, rest on the primordial fact that individuals are able to make shared sense (culture) of their circumstances and act on the shared sense they make. He wanted to know how this works and hit on the notion that people used shared methods of practical reasoning to build this shared sense of their common context of action and of the social world. Garfinkel argued that coordinated and meaningful actions, regardless of whether they involve cooperation or conflict, are impossible without this shared understanding. Thus any conception of social action is incomplete without an analysis of how social actors use shared common-sense knowledge and methods of reasoning in the conduct of their joint affairs. Garfinkel insisted that shared sense-making is a primordial feature of the social world. Nothing can happen in the social world without it. His project – ethnomethodology – was to study how socially shared methods of practical reasoning are used to analyse, understand and act in the commonsense world of everyday life.

British culture, through its invisible workings, allows the DoEAs and the DoSOs to have a shared understanding of their relationship to one another and to act on the shared sense they make: white superiority and black inferiority. This idea is confirmed by Mead's (1934) theory of the two dimensional self and its relationship to community (cited in Buccholz and Rosenthal, 1998). Mead argues that the individual is part of the social process and not an isolatable atomic being, as many might think. She explains this by encouraging us to think of a football team and how effectively they function together with each player knowing not only their own role but also the roles of all the other players in the team. Society is structured in more or less the same way. We see this in gendered roles, for example, where men and women are aware of their own roles as well as the roles of the other. The same is true for the roles of blacks and whites; each is aware of their own role expectations as well as the role of the other. There is a shared sense of relationship that is routinely acted on in everyday life. This is the reason why Buccholz and Rosenthal (1998) acknowledge that there is no such thing as black and white identities but that they are social products created in the moment of inter-action between members of the two groups. Mead, in detailing the features of the two dimensions of the self: the unique and creative 'I' and the traditional and conforming 'me' acknowledges individually different responses to this common shared sense achieved through processes of shared socialisation.

As a result of the insights gained through this research I could identify key mechanisms of the institution of social interaction that work to maintain and perpetuate the black-white duality, and the old psychological contract which was established between whites and blacks during slavery which I seek to interrupt in different ways.

Social Distance Strategies of the Institution of Social Interaction

The cultural rules I became aware of underpinning the institution of social interaction where race is concerned are shared in this section. I engage with these social distance strategies as a means of transforming my own mind-world and therefore thinking towards the goal of conscious bicultural com-petence. Schein (1978) acknowledges the main purpose of cultural rules is to avoid crippling anxiety of uncertainty and unpredictability through the 'routinisation of emotional responses'. We are largely unaware of these social distance strategies which tend to be over-learned and automatically applied and witnessed in the black-white duality. They occur beyond conscious awareness and act as the hidden controls of British culture (social distance boundary line drawings), operating on both the DoEAs and DoSOs to keep us in an oppositional relationship with one another as blacks and whites. In so doing they work effectively to maintain the current *status quo*. Smith (1991) refers to the social distance boundary lines (psychological defenses) used by ethnic groups to deal with historical conflicts they would rather not confront because they have been repressed or because they cause the individual or the group extreme anxiety. The social distance strategies that I have come to re-cognise are familiar to both the DoEAs and DoSOs as seen in Figure 6.3 opposite.

Figure 6.3: Social Distancing Strategies Maintaining Black-White Boundaries

Race	Race Taboo	Racialised Emotions	White Silence	Black Complicity
Ethnic Loyalties	Rhetorical Ethic	Political Correctness	Government Policy of Containment	Black Socialisation

Each of these is discussed in more depth here:

Race

Race, in terms of superior whites and inferior blacks is the major social distancing strategy, a strategy *par excellence* in that it has been kept in place effectively at an invisible level through British culture. A key function of culture is that of social stratification. Over the years I have discerned that it is not that I am not wanted in Britain as a black individual but that I must know my predetermined place in the present social order as it relates to the DoEAs in relation to the DoSOs. Placing race at the heart of British culture and embedding within it black and white cultures, beyond the level of conscious awareness, is also a significant social distance boundary line. This means that the differential black and white cultural socialisation will also take place beyond the level of conscious awareness. Chisom and Washington (1997) define race as:

> ... a specious classification of human beings created by Europeans (whites) which assigns human worth and social status using white as the model of humanity and the height of human achievement for the purpose of establishing and maintaining privilege and power.

Race Taboo

The shutting down of any attempt to discuss race as an issue as seen in the race taboo works to create extreme anxiety in any individual who touches the subject. This enables race as a social distance boundary line drawing to continue its work silently at the invisible level. Consequently discussion of the black body and what it signifies in the white imagination as a dimension of the human being becomes blocked as fears, doubts and anxieties are repressed through the felt need to conform.

Racialised Emotions

Racialised emotions (Martinas, 1992) are the outcome of the race taboo in that the individual is forced to push within themselves the emotional responses that cannot be openly acknowledged for fear of being punished or ostracised. Racialised emotions being repressed, instead of worked through, are stored in the individual like a bubbling cauldron threatening to boil over at any point. As a result the black individual spends most of his or her time managing these emotions in the presence of whites, leaving little energy for achieving academic excellence. In the main DoEAs have to manage their emotions in the presence of the DoSOs, as their ancestors did in slavery, enabling the DoSOs free to go about their business. Racialised emotions in whites occur then they feel threatened by the fear of the DoEAs releasing their emotional response to the black experience and so giving expression to black frustrations.

White silence

Racialised emotions (Martinas, 1992) are further triggered by the self-per-ceived need to protect one's own emotional well-being and to ensure that race as a social distance boundary line does its work effectively and silently. As a result the DoSOs generally adhere to the race taboo by maintaining white silence around the issues. This is necessary because since the subject of race is salient to the DoEAs, DoEAs are likely to ignore their emotional anxiety to pursue it since, as in my case, it actually became a life or death issue. White silence on the subject can work effectively to foil attempts to raise the subject and in the process leave DoEAs confused and fearful of being ostracised by the more powerful whites. White silence may well be supported by the adop-tion of a colour-blind approach to issues of race. Those DoSOs who are will-ing and able to violate the taboo have undergone a process to be able to do this, as seen in Helms' (1991) racial identity models.

Black complicity

The workings of race as a social construct, the race taboo and white silence invariably result in black complicity on the part of some DoEAs as a means of self-protection or to make personal gains in a white culture of power.

Ethnic loyalties

The idea of racism (with legislation to embed the idea in society) as an irra-tional urge is identified as the culprit of black problems. This is as opposed to the real issue of white ethnic loyalties. Kotkins (1993, 1996) reveals ethnicity to be critical to geopolitical power in the world. DoEAs are consequently mis-led to believe that their skin colour is the problem whereas it is what their skin colour signifies in the white imagination, a threat to the ethnic *status quo* and possible conflict is the real problem. In this way the DoEAs are left confused.

Rhetorical ethic

The rhetorical ethic defined by Ani (1994) as culturally structured hypocrisy designed to disarm the 'racial other' is another important social interaction mechanism. In England ethics primarily extend to those who are of one's own racial group – white culture. This is irrespective of what the legislation says and is frequently used as a cloaking device. The rhetorical ethic can be seen in ideas such as the existence of a meritocracy for all, equal opportunities and justice for all. DoEAs buying into the rhetorical ethic become even more confused.

Political correctness

Political correctness strengthens the race taboo by not allowing certain topics to be raised in polite company. Given the conformist nature of most DoEAs they will adhere to the political correctness rule even when it works against their own interests. This is especially the case since the DoEAs do not identify ethnically but are in fact situated at the margins of English society as 'one of the family' but in a subordinated relationship to whites (Hill Collins, 2001). Gorski (1995) acknowledges political correctness as a strategy used by closet racists who fear being identified as racists and so developed political correctness as a system in which everyone knows what to say in order to avoid having to walk on egg shells.

Control of education and government policy of containment

Control of the education of the DoEAs by the DoSOs who automatically and unthinkingly live out these social distance boundary line strategies could be seen as the final nail in the coffin ensuring white domination over blacks. A government policy of containment also ensures that problems such as race and black underachievement never are resolved because of the likely impact on vested interests. Critics have identified government as merely throwing some money at the problem and setting up commission after commission in order to placate the group (Cashmore, 1989; Gurnah, 1987).

Black socialisation

The distinctive black socialisation processes used by both the DoEAs and the DoSOs to inculturate DoEAs into black culture.

All of these mechanisms work to silence and block discussion of the issues. The ingenuity of the human mind means that the social distance strategies identified here will change form to perpetuate themselves – as they have done since the abolition of the slave trade and slavery – into newer and more subtle forms. For this reason consciousness is important if we are to transcend the black-white binary divide and not continue in the dark age of slavery.

These defensive routines (Putnam, 1993) – habitual ways of interacting to protect us or others from the threat of embarrassment – became apparent to me as I became adept at using the 'it makes sense' model (Bravette, 1996) shared in chapter seven. The use of defensive routines, which take on a life of their own, can also prevent organisational learning. This is especially the case when individuals experience them as an external force imposed by the situation and other players. Whites and blacks, the DoEAs and the DoSOs, have today been born into this complex, intricate and evolving social interaction order which is working to maintain the unequal cultural *status quo* between the two groups. The DoEAs are unable to make the breakthroughs they desire because of their lack of awareness that black socialisation is externally administered and mediated by the DoSOs and is happening beyond their conscious awareness. The deafening silence surrounding the group experience of the DoEAs by institutional agents congruently embedded in organisations functioning as neopigmentocracies means there are limited possibilities of adopting the inter-group approach to managing diversity in organisational life recommended by Alderfer. When I use inter-group theory and frame my concerns within the institutional context as that of a DoEA seeking to correct historical wrongs which are still evident today, a sincere theory of groups in a multicultural society/organisation would take this on board instead of using social distance strategies such as silence and denial.

Understanding the black-white duality in more depth

In studying these mechanisms we are able to see the mutual process in which the DoSOs and DoEAs are both caught up. It becomes evident that it is no longer appropriate for the DoEAs to continue to blame the DoSOs – because this means giving away our own personal power to bring about change for ourselves. Focussing instead on our role as social actors in the maintenance of the current *status quo* where the white-black relationship is concerned opens up new possibilities. Because our roles have typically been passive and subordinated we have failed to realise that we are still actors who are crucial to the racial drama being enacted. Awareness of the social interaction institution make it possible for us to begin the work of interrupting dysfunctional patterns of behaviour in ourselves and through a ripple effect interrupting them in others. As Gergen (1994) notes: 'Who is to blame, since if I change my role, does not the taken for granted role of other social actors also become interrupted?'

What becomes apparent is that the DoEAs are as culpable as the DoSOs in perpetuating the black-white binary divide in the 21st century. For example, I realised that as a DoEA I had unwittingly bought into the ideology of race because of my unconsciousness and was emphatic in identifying myself as black without clearly understanding its deeper implications. Being black I could only ever see myself relative to whites, as their inferior, as this is projected onto me. I had also been deeply indoctrinated into adhering to the race taboo because I had become normalised to white silence and denial on issues related to race. The impact of managing emotions that have been racialised also acted as a strong force which resulted in apathy and ambivalence on my part, especially in the face of collusive white responses. DoEAs, in a state of unconsciousness as a group, are likely to be in denial and avoidance where race is concerned as an issue in British society.

Analysis of the institution of slavery

It is interesting that although so many people discuss slavery, little written analysis has been done on how the institution of slavery worked and continues to work today in the global economy. Analysis of the institution of chattel slavery based on the work of Hiro (1971), Patterson (1973, 1982) and Elkins (1968) highlights certain characteristic features. These will be described so that they can be considered for their overall impact on transforming and maintaining the enslaving and slave personalities, as seen in the symbiotic relationship between the DoSOs and DoEAs. They can also be studied to gain understanding of the extent to which they can still be recognised in modern societies like Britain today. Culture as process is endlessly adaptive, emanates from the creative thinking of the human being and works to perpetuate itself in a variety of forms. The institution of slavery served the English well. Consequently there was no need, from their perspective, to get rid of it. Its five features are shown in Figure 6.4:

Figure 6.4: Characteristic Features of the Institution of Slavery

- A closed system
- Accommodationist behaviours
- Culture of passivity
- Divided/fragmented group dynamics
- White absenteeism

A closed system

This is seen in the workings of the interactional order in which blacks find themselves. Enslaved Africans were taken from their natural environment and placed in a closed system in the middle of the Atlantic where they were subjected to a socialisation process administered by whites. This process, known as 'seasoning', was designed to transform their psychology. In similar ways in the 21st century the DoEAs find themselves culturally isolated from their roots and trapped in the closed system of British culture which on the whole they do not understand. The system was and is closed in that literally all avenues of escape are closed off and the DoEAs are trapped in the black-white duality in their mind-world. Within this closed system they are forced to conform or be marginalised.

Accommodationist behaviours

In order to avoid the damage the workings of the interactional order can cause for the DoEAs they acquiesce to its demands instead of confronting or negotiating with it. Having been inculturated into an inferior culture within British culture the DoEAs continue to be unconsciously dependent on their previous masters. In my own case I was fearful of thinking my own thoughts according to my own consciousness because of the extent to which they conflicted with what the DoSOs told me about myself as a black person. Instead I sought to accommodate the DoSOs in every way because with the closed system of British culture I feared for my safety, well-being and survival. Over the span of my life in Britain I have witnessed white power-holders exerting their authority over my life chances as a black woman and those of my children in a variety of ways. My conformity was demanded.

Culture of passivity

The closed system and demand for accommodation results in a culture of passivity, poverty, deprivation and soul murder for the DoEAs. Black culture is itself designed to be a culture of passivity and deprivation as enslaved Africans subordinated themselves to the demands of whites with the only other alternative being death. In modern society for many blacks death can be correlated with a loss of livelihood given their vulnerable status in the secondary labour market. These conditions have their consequences for group life.

Divided/fragmented group dynamics

The foregoing features placed immense strain on the ability of the physically and psychologically enslaved to take care of the needs of their own families. Allegiances instead become focused on the DoSOs and the benefits to be gained from fostering these relationships especially when favour and patronage is found from whites. Within the institution of slavery whites had absolute power over blacks and not even black family relationships were sacrosanct. Allegiances between the DoEAs continue to be divided today as many jockey against one another for white patronage. Having created this institution the slave-owners then absented themselves (physically) from it.

White absenteeism

Even though slave-owners were responsible for putting these dynamics in place they absented themselves physically and psychologically from the institution. Silence is an example of absenteeism in that it hides thoughts and emotions that would reveal their unconscious bicultural competence to themselves and their conscious bicultural competence to others. The victim is then blamed. This quality can be seen in Gorski's (1995) idea of 'disownership' as one of the three language indicators of a closet racist, the other two being fear and unawareness. It is also evident in Bergenhenegouwen's (1987) idea of the institutionalisation of distrust and detachment, as seen in so many organisations.

These five characteristic features can be used, alongside the social distance strategies of the social interaction order, as a lens of analysis investigating the extent to which the institution of slavery continues to thrive in our lives today. The closed system can be seen in the discussion of culture as inner experience where the DoSOs are shown to dominate my inner world as a result of the black-white duality into which I was trapped. The vignettes from my life and the literature also confirm the experience of being trapped in a closed system. The knock-on outcomes, as seen in the other four characteristics, become more easily understandable when a closed system is effectively in place. The shared understanding and rules of British culture into which I had been unconsciously socialised left me confused and complicit. Understanding these processes facilitates our movement from a place of unconsciousness to a place of consciousness. Elkins (1968) identifies the antidote to slavery as that of creating margins of space and enabling the slave individual to know that they have a real and valued contribution that matters to make. These themes are taken up in chapter ten.

Generative educators

In this chapter we learn about culture as process, and see how the DoEAs have been positioned in British society in relation to the white ethnic majority and other ethnic minority groups. In understanding talk-in-interaction and the institution of social interaction we have gained important insights into how culture as process works. The social distance mechanisms used to maintain the wall of silence erected between whites and blacks which are working to maintain the *status quo* are also revealed. As teachers we are offered further means of intervention in the process of dismantling the racial *status quo* of inequality between DoEAs and DoSOs by contradicting our own roles in the normalised and taken-for-granted social distance mechanisms as we participate in the institution of social interaction. In the next chapter I discuss how this knowledge gave me insights into how my inner culture was being un-consciously shaped by British culture. I also offer insights of the steps I have taken to counteract the dysfunctions I found, enabling me to work through the conflicts I experienced in terms of my technical generativity as described in the introduction.

7

Culture as inner experience:
silent power

It is our unnoticed culture that manipulates us as an individual as well as a society ... (Newman, 2002)

That I feed the beggar; that I forgive an insult, that I love my enemy ... all these are undoubtedly great virtues ... But what if I should discover that the least amongst them all, the poorest of the beggars, the most impudent of all offenders, yea the very fiend himself – that these are within me, and that I myself stand in need of the alms of my own kindness, that I myself am the enemy who must be loved – what then? (Jung, 1938)

Some of the groups in society that are most vulnerable to becoming victims of social exclusion are forgotten simply because not enough is known about their particular circumstances. (ONS, 2003)

Introduction

Applying knowledge to my everyday experience throughout the research helped me to realise the nature of culture and how it becomes
inner experience and to see the implications of this for both the DoEAs and DoSOs. I came to understand the psychic disorientation, social amnesia, confusion and despair which underpinned my life as the lack of inner inte-gration that slave masters wanted to foster in the slaves they were creating in the Caribbean. This would ensure our dependency and subservience. The fact that these themes continue to be underlying features of the culture of blacks, as enslaved Africans were renamed on the plantations, suggests that the mechanism put in place during slavery continues to work silently and effectively. The internalised intra-psychic outcomes of British culture crystal-lised as I researched my history and realised the oppositional nature of the

black-white relationship laid bare in this chapter. In the process I came to understand myself as a DoEA and not as 'black'. This meant that my opposite, 'whites', were not whites at all but the DoSOs. This led to my decision to rename myself as what I am, a DoEA, and to drop the conferred and fore-closed black identity. Use of the identifiers 'DoEAs' and 'DoSOs' clarifies the issues surrounding race. At the same time it interrupts the workings of the institution of social interaction.

Black socialisation externally administered

Thanks to the knowledge being developed and the processes I was under-going I realised that I am the recipient of black socialisation, internally and externally administered. I gradually came to understand that as a black person I was living within the boundaries of white culture and its privilege as an onlooker but denied entry to it. In addition, I was constantly being pushed into an inferior mode of life. Through this persistent positioning of the DoEAs in relation to the DoSOs we are effectively socialised by the DoSOs into black culture, which is a culture of poverty and deprivation. Black socialisation refers to inferior socialisation designed to maintain power differentials be-tween enslaved Africans and their descendants and slaveholders and their descendants. Black socialisation naturally results in black culture which is an inferior design for living. In short, the research process reveals the black prob-lem as a British cultural inheritance.

Further inquiry was necessary on how the black socialisation that occurs at the hands of whites as the DoSOs and which flows through white culture is unwittingly supported by the black socialisation of the DoEAs. For example how am I complicit in my own oppression? That this is the case is seen most clearly in the vignettes presented in chapter three: it is the DoSOs operating as institutional agents who define what it means for me to be black and who place limits around my aspirations as a DoEA. Black socialisation at the hands of whites describes the various means the DoSOs use to maintain social dis-tance between themselves and what they consider to be their possessions and the DoEAs. This is true of jobs, reward packages or other resources and underpins the neopigmentocracy.

DoEAs as a cultural inheritance

Whether the DoSOs overtly recognise and acknowledge this to be so or not, the evidence suggests that blacks, the DoEAs, are a visible legacy of slavery, bequeathed to them by their ancestors to service their needs and society as subordinated members of English culture. I do not use the term racism be-cause what is termed race discrimination is in reality the ethnic discrimination and subordination of enslaved Africans in relation to Caucasians as determined during slavery. The total subordination of the enslaved African was ensured in a way that was not achieved with those who were colonised but not subjected to extended enslavement. Critical to understanding the black-white relationship is also the idea of a neo-colonial relationship, discussed in the previous chapter, working to maintain master-slave dynamics. Ani (1994) does not overstate her point when she writes of the weapon of culture, because culture is used as an invisible weapon that continues to maintain the black-white binary division in the world: it is internalised by both blacks and whites as normal and part and parcel of the human experience.

Black culture internally administered

Black culture, a culture of deprivation and soul murder (Painter, 1995; Young, 2000) victimhood (Pinderhughes, 1979), and an externally imposed cultural disorder (McWhorter, 2001), consists of the erroneous belief systems instilled into enslaved Africans through the processes of seasoning and the ongoing treatment needed to maintain the black-white social order in slavery. Enslaved Africans adapted this culture on a day-to-day basis to ease the conditions of their lives where they could. However, there is no evidence of black culture being reviewed post-slavery to ensure its generativity. What we find instead is that the historical subordination of the DoEAs to the DoSOs as a survival and self-protection strategy is also unwittingly maintained and transmitted through black culture.

The inner culture that accrues from black socialisation and culture

Engaging with my own mind-world as a means of resolving my own crisis of meaning threw up the themes detailed in Figure 7.1 as significant and ongoing, which I needed to engage with systematically and deliberately:

Figure 7.1: Culture as Inner Experience

Introjected White Consciousness	Black Consciousness
Whites as primary referent point	Self-denial/fear of self
Fear of whites and their possible misuse of power and/or white backlash	Lack of self-knowledge and self-awareness
	Silent and silenced/shame and shamed
White silence/collusion/race taboo	Enslaved and colonised mind
White social distance strategies	Complicity, collusion due to isolation
Need to protect white interests	Loss of spontaneity and creativity
	Psychosomatic illnesses

Figure 7.1 reveals my mind-world as split in two, warring between the concerns of the DoSOs and my own concerns as a DoEA, and with my own concerns subordinated to those of the DoSOs. I found the answer to the question I asked in chapter two: why were whites so important to me whereas I was so unimportant to them? Where was the mutuality in our relationship? The ongoing normalised internalised black-white chatter that had become second nature to me, so that I was largely unaware of it, showed that I had internalised the split between the white and black worlds with whites dominating in my mind-world. It was an ongoing process of the subjugation of the mind resulting in the subservient character traits necessary for survival in British society (Holdt, 2002). This inner experience had come to a head as a result of working in a large higher education institution where the black-white binary division had been institutionalised and was routinely enacted. As I became aware of the issues and sought to articulate them I found myself being hushed, marginalised, ignored, left feeling invisible and ultimately vulnerable and highly expendable.

DuBois' double consciousness in practice

Figure 7.1 is in effect the double consciousness, conceptualised by DuBois (1903) at the beginning of the 20th century, acknowledging the deep-seated conflicts within the psychological world of the DoEAs as they live and work within a white superior culture that simultaneously devalues and inferiorises them on the basis of their skin colour and race. DuBois (1903) wrote of 'a veil' in which the DoEAs have 'no true self-consciousness' because they are only allowed to see themselves 'through the revelation of the other world'. I had been trying to prove to whites something that I already was: good enough as a human being, something I had not been socialised to know in Britain. The persistent denial of my reality by otherwise seemingly sane and intelligent significant others (like teachers) worked to confuse me, causing me to question my own ability to interpret and make sense of reality. The outcomes acknowledged in my inner experience replicate the experiences detailed in earlier chapters of this book but without my awareness of how this had come about and is maintained. What I realised was that whites and blacks internalise British culture differentially depending on whether we are the recipients of white or black socialisation. Figure 7.2 opposite depicts how this works.

DoSOs internalise a perspective where it is a normalised experience to understand themselves as superior to the DoEAs. DoEAs, on the other hand, internalise a perspective where it is a normalised experience to understand themselves to be inferior to and dependant on the DoSOs. DoSOs in many

Figure 7.2 White and Black Mind-Worlds

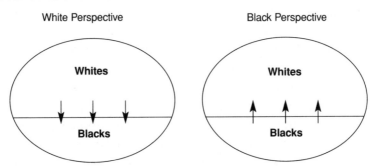

ways nurture this dependency. British culture is the architecture that holds this arrangement in place, consisting of black and white subcultures. The black culture that the DoEAs so strenuously defend is seen to lack cultural integrity given that it is an English creation used to manage the diversity of the empire while maintaining power differentials between the two groups.

Significantly, whites also internalise this double consciousness which allows them to eclipse blacks and other non-whites to a lesser extent as if they are non-existent and therefore unimportant, non-members of the human race. Simultaneously, blacks are dysfunctionally tied to whites because of their internalised dependence on them.

These insights gained from deliberate and systematic engagement with what it means for me to be black initially raised more questions than they answered. Was my inner self my inner self or was it an introjected white consciousness masquerading as my inner self? Could I even trust my own knowing anymore? I began to see how my inner world had been unwittingly subordinated to whites to get by and survive in British society where I live as an outsider, devalued and inferiorised because of the dynamics shown in Figure 7.2. Buying into the lie of the social construct of what it means to be black I had internalised erroneous belief systems that had effectively turned me against myself, even as I instinctually struggled against this. I had shut down on myself in order to survive. Had I begun to perceive some of these ways of being in my own children, suggesting unconscious intergenerational transmission of unarticulated values, belief systems and coping strategies? The DoEAs who experience the material conflict between the black and white worlds in a state of unconsciousness must live it out in their internal world because of the workings of the race taboo, white silence and collusion around issues of race.

Psychological contracts

The psychological contract that evolves from the arrangement seen in Figure 7.2 is therefore not mutually agreed. The idea of psychological contracts, borrowed from the human resource discipline, helps to understand the black-white relationship. Psychological contracts are unwritten implicit mutual expectations between two groups. They develop and evolve through interactions and experiences taking the form of a mental model or schema that people use to interpret their world and generate appropriate behaviours. The evidence suggests that there is not a mutually agreed or shared psychological contract between blacks and whites in Britain. The practice of white silence masks this fact. Although psychological contracts implied in British society suggest equality of opportunity, fairness, justice and the existence of a meritocracy the reality in terms of the white mindset revealed in Figure 7.2 shows the opposite. In my own research the psychological contract that revealed itself operating beyond our conscious awareness in the mind-world of the DoSOs is the old psychological contract (see figure 7.3 below) that evolved during slavery and into which the DoEAs are socialised via black socialisation externally administered by whites. The DoEAs, on the other hand, inevitably develop and evolve a confused psychological contract as they are caught between:

- the contradictions of the old psychological contract being unconsciously externally imposed

- our own desires based on the espoused social contract of the equality of opportunity, justice and meritocracy

- the rhetorical ethic

The gap between the well-intentioned but confused psychological contract of the DoEAs and the old one held by the DoSOs from the arrangements of the institution of slavery is vast. In the chasm between these two sets of expectations of the other the oppositional black-white duality is forged, enacted and re-enacted. The masked and silenced contract held by the DoSOs is significantly different from the explicit contract that underpins the espoused values of British society and culture. The same contradiction was witnessed in British culture which claimed freedom as its most important value and yet enslaved so many.

Old and new psychological contracts

Figure 7.3 acknowledges the chasm between the old psychological contract that currently exists between the DoEAs and the DoSOs and the new psychological contract I began to create in my own mind-world as the expectations

I had to have of myself in terms of my relationship with other DoEAs and DoSOs. This is the legacy that I am now working at passing on to the young of the DoEAs and is designed to undermine the dysfunctions discussed throughout. The old psychological contract existing between the DoEAs and the DoSOs as an invisible legacy of slavery is juxtaposed against the new psychological contract I developed for myself in Figure 7.3 below:

Figure 7.3: Old and New Psychological Contracts

The old psychological contract:	The new psychological contract:
■ Between blacks and whites	■ Between the British-English and BACs
■ Needs black and white cultures resulting in differential black and white socialisation processes and consciousnesses.	■ Needs distinct English and BAC cultures ensuring cultural integrity for each group
■ Depends on unconscious assimilation into British culture via black socialisation	■ Depends on the bicultural socialisation of BACs (DoEAs) and the DoSOs
■ Based on ongoing master-slave relationship	■ Based on cultural integrity
■ Controlled by whites by way of black-white duality	■ Mutual relationship between BAC and the ethnic majority
■ Blacks are unconscious and dependent on whites	■ BACs are conscious and independent of the ethnic majority

Before I negotiated this new psychological contract with DoSOs I had to find my new identity as a BAC myself rather than risking yet another form of imposition by the DoSOs. The new psychological contract works to dismantle the internalised black-white duality – and therefore psychological slavery, resulting from the old psychological contract. In the process of this change I exist in the murky world of becoming British African-Caribbean even though whites continue to treat me as a black.

The black-white duality

The black-white duality is an invisible legacy of slavery and I define it as the oppositional internalised symbiotic inferior/superior dynamic relationship that exists between the descendants of enslaved Africans and the descendants of slave-owners. The dynamic was put in place during slavery and has been institutionalised within British culture (with its black and white sub-cultures) as the means by which the fixed power differentials between the two groups are maintained over time.

This relationship is best understood as the experiences contained in Figures 7.1 and 7.2. Buccholz and Buccholz (1998) provide important insights into how the black-white duality works dynamically when they argue that there is no such thing as black and white identities, rather they are the social products of interactions between the DoSOs and the DoEAs. Surfacing the black-white duality directed me to the imperative of destabilising the dominance of white consciousness in my internal world. The black-white duality, when acknowledged and understood, can be witnessed at work in relationships between blacks and whites throughout the world. The symbiotic nature of the black-white duality also reveals why the DoEAs use the DoSOs as natural comparators unlike ethnic minorities who use members of their own group to compare themselves against (Ogbu, 1997). As a result of these findings references to blacks and whites throughout the text refer to those who own these labels because they are unconsciously trapped in the workings of the black-white duality.

The black-white duality as a disease

Skillings and Dobbins' (1991) conceptualisation of racism as a disease that affects both the perpetuators and the target group can also be seen in the black-white duality. They use an addictions model to understand what they term racism but which also explains the black-white duality.

> The addiction is to a world view that is used by the host to support a sense of emotional well-being and avoid cognitive dissonance and emotional pain. The addiction is in large part supported by a schema of irrelevance, which excludes data that challenge that sense of well-being. (p211)

DoEAs and DoSOs who are locked in the black-white duality are seen to be addicted to their world views of differential black and white cultures, consciousnesses and identities. This black-white duality underpins the experiences detailed in chapters three and four in the relationship between DoEAs and DoSOs and is acknowledged in the organisational context and in helping services such as mental health. The black-white duality can be likened to Pavlov's experimentation in behaviour modification with the dog in terms of how it functions. The black and white identifiers operate like the bell triggering automatic responses in the dog in anticipation of meat appearing. In the case of blacks and whites it is anticipation of conflict occurring.

Process issues

Engaging with the process issues culminating from the findings of Figures 7.1, 7.2 and 7.3, with the aim of transforming my life, was immensely challenging as I began the journey of living consciously instead of unconsciously and automatically. I soon realised why the choice of unconsciousness is so easy: I did not have to take responsibility for myself or for the social setting in which I lived. I could simply blame God or whites, anyone else but myself. Engaging with the process of living consciously, while applying knowledge to my life, was a messy, uncertain, chaotic, scary and risky process. My comfort zones were challenged as required actions revealed the dysfunctions of the choices I had previously been making.

In writing about the experience I have ordered and structured experiences and events so as to ease understanding but the actual process was nothing of the sort. It involved taking huge risks, like questioning my faith, then jumping back in shock and fear of my world collapsing around me if I proceeded. I frequently stopped short in the research, fearful of going any further. Many times I found myself going backwards in my actions even as the new insights were challenging my mind-world. Coming upon new leads, going in new directions, making links with what I had left behind, returning to old ground but with new eyes and new perspectives. I acknowledge these themes because I know that the normal human defence mechanism will seek to bypass them where possible, as I would still do if I could. But this would stymie the transformation process, which is so essential for the DoEAs to move beyond our current status. Underlying all the themes outlined in Figure 7.1 were significant emotional responses ranging from shock, deeply felt pain, psychosomatic illnesses, tears and anger to fear, sadness, grief and self-blame: how could I have been so stupid! These feelings are a constant underlying theme of the process I underwent as I worked with the unconsciousness of my bi-cultural awareness which I discerned as the fundamental problem in my life as a DoEA.

Resolving the specific issues surfaced did not occur at one specific time but took many years to achieve. I spent years engaging in first person action research with the goal of self-transformation before I moved on to engage others in second and third person action research as I sought to gain deeper insights into what it means to be black in Britain. The theme of silence and shame is used as an illustration of how I have dealt with the thirteen themes indicated in Figure 7.1.

Engaging with silence and shame
Working with the silence and the resultant shame that surrounded my life experience as a black woman required me to first accept and make the commitment to engage with the theme to witness how it actually worked itself out in my life. Individual and group reflection was supported by a survey of the literature before planning an action to be carried out in various settings. In

the main such actions were mainly challenges to myself to break the collusive silences I maintained in a self-protective stance. As I moved to carry out my planned action different variables would emerge which enabled me to understand the factors that either supported or prevented me from achieving my goals. Another period of individual and collaborative reflection would occur before moving on to another cycle of planned action, observation, reflection and re-planning. The process of working with my own internalised silences and the resultant shame allowed me to understand the political nature of an experience which I had internalised as personal.

The themes in Figure 7.1 interwove as I worked with each one: they are not mutually exclusive so at any one time I could be working with a number of different themes simultaneously. Over time my insights about how silence and shame were working themselves out in my daily life deepened. To date I have worked with this theme to the extent that I am no longer uncomfortable with silences: I understand how they work and have released myself from shame as a negative emotional response. I now know that silence and shame about slavery is not a personal but a group phenomenon and that we need to move beyond it emotionally. Unsurfaced, the silence and resultant shame surrounding this historical event had been working to cripple me in ways of which I was unaware.

As I researched I became aware of how a culture of silence pervades western cultures like Britain and America (Winton, 2003). Lukes (1974) links silence with power, acknowledging that people often become complicit in their own oppression and thus help to sustain it. Power is used to shape 'perceptions, cognitions and preferences in such a way that people accept their role in the existing order of things because they can see or imagine no alternative to it, because they view it as natural and unchangeable or because they value it as divinely preordained and beneficial' (Lukes, 1974: 24).

The power of socialisation

Cycles of action research and inquiry revealed that silence is a function of society and is alternatively understood as cultural censorship as seen in the race taboo. In my own case there is a requirement on me to be complicit in not acknowledging my identity as a DoEA in the institutional context let alone articulate the legitimate concerns I carry as a member of this group. This confirms why Alderfer's inter-group theory (see chapter three) is not used practically in organisations. For me to be respected in the context of my group experience as a DoEA could lead to widespread transformations if the white ethnic majority recognised the working through of this history as important.

I also identified shame and internalised oppression as classic symptoms of silence. Jews have identified the conspiracy of silence that exists between Germans and Jews (Dasberg, 1991) but the silence between blacks and whites has yet to be acknowledged. I was struggling with the difficulty of speaking my own mind in a culture that conspires to deny and silence my knowledge as a black woman seeking to speak from within that experience. Interestingly, Matsuura (2004) refers to the enforced dialogue brought about by slavery. But power relations between blacks and whites ensure that any such dialogue is effectively silenced through the hidden controls of British culture. Despite extensively researching the subject of silence I did not include it in any significant way in my written PhD thesis. By taking the research path of engaging with white silences as sources of data about the workings of the race taboo I came to understand how much of my complicit silences were about protecting white interests even when these were detrimental to my own interests. Matsuura (2004) is right about the deafening silence that prevents understanding of the impact of slavery not only on the geography of the world but on black and white interactions at the micro level today.

Sainsbury's Centre for Mental Health (SCMH, 2002) provides some insights into this culture of fear both on the part of DoEAs and the DoSOs stemming from the fear and distrust they feel of each other and which ultimately results in silenced dialogue. The DoSO's fear is likely to be based on the stereotypical images they have of the DoEAs as a group. There is also the view that DoSOs fear possible accusations of racism and clamp up when these issues arise taking a self-protective stance. Mental health professionals admit to not being able to talk about issues of race and culture because of fear of the subject. Jacob Holdt (2002) points out that the most destructive form of racism, understood as black socialisation for the DoEAs, is what the DoSOs hold in their thoughts about them as blacks as these are internalised by the victims. He also argues that racism is far more destructive than poverty in that poverty does not destroy the initiative and self-reliance of a people which racism or black socialisation at the hands of DoSOs does.

The crucial question for me was: whose interests were my silences serving? How far would and could I go in breaking silence around issues of race? As a child I had been socialised to be completely dependent on the DoSOs: I had been socialised to fear them. Ongoing black socialisation via the media also confirms the power the DoSOs have over the lives of the DoEAs. Institutionally, this power is enacted as a matter of course. In these ways the DoEAs have been forced to place faith in the DoSOs with most of our lives preoccupied in finding the ways and means to accommodate them so that we can survive while holding onto our jobs and livelihood where possible. We are regularly reminded that this is not our country suggesting that I am only here because the DoSOs allow me to be: as a black individual I have no rights despite what my espoused status as a British citizen

Choices: from inauthentic to authentic

Laing (1961) writes about the game of collusion that people play as in the way blacks and whites collude together based on the old psychological contract: this perpetuates white superiority and black inferiority. I finally concluded that my shame was the shame of unconsciously participating in this game of collusion. Laing (1961:111) notes:

> Collusion is always clinched when self finds in other that other who will 'confirm' self in the false self that is trying to make real and vice versa. The ground is then set for prolonged mutual evasion of truth and true fulfilment. Each has found an other to endorse her own false notion of herself and to give this appearance a semblance of reality.

Whyte (1994) expands on this idea in relation to the workplace where he observes that the split between what is nourishing at work and what is agonising is the chasm from which our personal destiny emerges. The movement of these latent energies within, fuelled by the research, had brought me to the need for honouring my inner world. I began the work necessary to facilitate a move from the dysfunctional black perspective portrayed in Figure 7.2 (p125) to the more life-enhancing stance of understanding myself as a British African-Caribbean (Skowron, 2004).

Figure 7.4: Becoming British African-Caribbean and Ending the Black-White Duality in my Mind-World

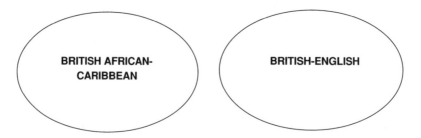

BRITISH AFRICAN-CARIBBEAN

BRITISH-ENGLISH

Figure 7.4 shows the decision I made to remove the black-white binary division from my inner culture by replacing it with all of me: British African-Caribbean. The BAC me is the me, unfettered by issues of race and black socialisation, who is reaching after self- actualisation. It is the me that exists hidden away under the weight and burden of black culture as externally imposed by whites and dysfunctionally internalised. Placing focus on me enabled me to begin to witness my life unfolding as me. In this way I was able to stop blaming the problems in my life on racism and so conforming to what Widdowson (2001) refers to as an age-old pattern of delusional thinking. Delusional thinking means that people pay attention only to the external causes of their troubles rather than deal with factors over which they have some control. Effectively, I changed my mind about myself, realising that the inner environment between my ears is mine and mine alone. I began to think more highly of myself with striking outcomes. I had begun the differentiation process that Stonequist (1961) states that blacks have not engaged with because of the nature of their relationship with whites. This brings to mind the senior white male colleague who publicly criticised me for being what he termed 'solipsistic' as I was struggling towards becoming important to myself – something the DoEAs are not socialised to be in British society. Removing whites from my inner culture was a means of ensuring cultural integrity as I tested the adage 'as within so without' for its truth.

I began to develop social intelligence and in so doing, in Gergen's (1994) view, to open up new possibilities for cultural life. I realised that in living in the midst of a network of reciprocating black-white identities, my identity as an inferior black can only be maintained as long as both whites and blacks play their proper supporting roles. I realised that the moment I chose to renege on the inferior black role I threaten the array of interdependent superior white constructions that surround me. In differentiating myself and taking on the British African-Caribbean identity I had arrived at an achieved identity gained through psychological maturation as opposed to the conferred and foreclosed black identity (Hoover *et al*, 1997) which had been externally imposed and uncomfortably taken on. I moved from unconscious to conscious in terms of the fixed black identity which had kept me locked into a dysfunctional relationship with whites as seen in Figure 7.5 below.

Figure 7.5: Bicultural Identity Matrix

	Unconscious	Conscious
Bicultural Identity Incompetence	Foreclosure – acceptance/no exploration (don't know I don't know)	Moratorium – in process (know I don't know)
Bicultural Identity Competence	Diffusion – confused and ambivalent (don't know I know)	Achievement – choice and awareness (know I know)

The research process reveals that institutional experiences related to race had caused me to move from a foreclosed to a diffused identity as I began to question what it meant for me to be black. My developing autobiographical awareness brought me to the moratorium stage with the acceptance of my British African-Caribbean antecedents. The result has been an achieved, albeit transitional, identity.

Adopting the human centred passionate appreciation approach

The challenge of working with the themes identified in this chapter was made easier by understanding that I had been culturally determined by other human beings to fit an image they wanted to hold of me in order to exploit my human capabilities for their own ends. The obvious response for me would be to gain insights into what it meant to be human before slavery. In the process I developed the human-centred passionate appreciation approach to working with myself. This counter-cultural approach now underpins my classroom practice. The re-engineering work I engaged with involved subordinating both external white and black voices of authority to the authority of my inner self-consciousness. I had started the process of learning to be my own person as opposed to what either blacks or whites were telling me I should be. I was able over time to move beyond black and white and begin the process of finding out what it actually means for me to be me. I was now engaging in authentic human development as I had broken through the veil of race. Engaging with what I had learnt from developing autobiographical awareness as well as what I was learning from the literature revealed to me the process through which I had settled into the role of being black in relation to whites. There were a whole host of beliefs, attitudes and behaviours that I was now going to have to contradict if I was to transform the dysfunctional experiences that had brought me to this research in the first place. In the next section I share the It Makes Sense model I developed to support this re-engineering work:

The It Makes Sense model

Systematic use of the 'It Makes Sense' model (Bravette, 1996), the strategy I devised and have used consistently as a means of working with the issues that arose, is essentially a self-re-education model. The model facilitated the re-orientation of my mindset while challenging me to be open to different perspectives.

Figure 7.6: It Makes Sense

Self-knowledge and self-awareness
It was necessary for me to develop self-knowledge and self-awareness about what it actually meant for me to be human as well as black, to know myself historically and culturally.

Education for critical consciousness
It was necessary for me to engage in self-re-education seeking out the knowledge I needed for myself as opposed to waiting for someone else to teach me.

Nurturing the internal world
It was necessary for me to honour and nurture my own internal world, the self that I had been systematically denying in order to gain acceptance in white culture.

Seeking support through networking
It was necessary for me to move beyond the silence and shame and therefore isolation I was experiencing about what it meant for me to be black to share with other human beings.

Embedding process in my life
It was necessary to accept that since most of my life had been a lie and that I had been ignorant about so many things that I now needed to hold truth lightly and to be open to the lessons brought to me by the processes in which I was now engaged.

To contradict the dysfunctions I found to be inherent to black life in Britain I found myself:

- Learning to value my own life as a DoEA and to know that despite this history I am worthwhile in myself as a human being

- Overturning the stigmatised identity into which I am moulded and socialised in British society through changing my mind about myself and in so doing proving to myself that black dysfunction is not genetic or biological but socially constructed

- Psychologically distancing myself from the DoSOs, enabling me to see that I have something of value to contribute to the world since this is not a way of being that the DoSOs typically socialise the DoEAs to understand.

- Re-naming myself on my own terms as the DoEAs so that I can find out what it means for me to be me, as revealed through my own historical journey and self-consciousness, has been another critical step towards developing an inner life.

- Re-humanising myself through engaging with the slavery experience and working with the psychological, spiritual, emotional, physical and cultural outcomes of this experience. Carrying out corrective surgery. Protecting my spiritual hygiene

- ■ Exchanging the race lens of analysis with a more generative human lens of analysis to understand the life experience of the DoEAs

- ■ Accepting that given our shared history DoSOs who are unconscious or ignorant of the issues discussed here are not in a position to participate in the socialisation of the DoEAs

These choices directly contradict white culture and facilitated my transition from a place of unconscious bicultural competence to that of conscious bicultural incompetence. Conscious bicultural competence, developed through engaging with my life experiences, enabled me to distinguish between the dysfunctional psychological contract developed to hold together the institution of slavery and the new psychological contract necessary to dismantling it. The new psychological contract required new belief systems, new values and new ways of being: it required a new culture underpinned by a *metanoia*.

Generative Educators

This chapter reveals how I went about working through the issues that the five-dimensional human being model in chapter five had surfaced for me as an individual. My research had conclusively led me to realise that to help my young I had to help myself: I had to work with my own life and provide a role model for how to work with the challenges that life will also inevitably present them. I began consciously engaging with myself as a human being who has responsibilities and integrities of her own to protect. This chapter gives examples of the deeply personal work which I had to engage with as a parent and educator to facilitate me to become fit for the purpose of teaching not just my own but other people's children. This is important for all of us as educators. In addition I surfaced important insights into the profound problems faced by the members of my group which had deepened substantially as had the urgency for something to be done about the experience described here.

Having successfully re-negotiated my status in British society I could see that this process was more widely needed for DoEAs and teachers in the education system. My vision is of parents and teachers who have developed their conscious bicultural competence enabling us to facilitate learners effectively into the process of becoming conscious creators of culture themselves. This is particularly important for us as DoEAs if we are to take back control of our own lives. Consequently, the next three chapters focus on how we can move forward into the future.

8

Developing conscious bicultural competence

To say that culture is constituted under the sign of hope is to say the injustices which deform each and every culture cannot be final, cannot be accepted as destiny. There is a strange new world towards which culture is directed, the theological symbol for which is the kingdom. Rather than culture as destiny, this according to the gospel, is the destiny of culture reached by the long revolution, the journey from bondage to freedom.
(Barth cited by Gorringe, 2004)

Consciousness is a fresh fruit of evolution and our most prized possession. It is consciousness that sets us apart from the opulent variety of earth-life and puts upon us an onus of responsibility. It takes us on incredible journeys and has given us the gifts of insight and transcendence. The same kind of process that gives the earth abundant life allows us to have a sense of self, to contemplate the world, to forecast the future and make ethical choices. Each of us has under our control a miniature world, continuously evolving, making constructs unique to our own minds. In the same way that life itself unfolded, our mental life is progressively enriched, enabling each of us to create our own world.
(Sarkar, 2001)

All the greatest and most important problems in life are fundamentally insoluable ... They can never be solved, but only outgrown. This 'outgrowing' proves on further investigation to require a new level of consciousness. Some higher or wider interest appeared on the horizon and through the broadening of outlook the insoluable problem lost its urgency. It was not solved logically in its own terms but faded when confronted with a new and stronger life urge.
(Carl Jung, 1938)

Introduction

The bicultural competence that accrues from bicultural socialisation, especially when used with the five dimensional human being model, is discussed in more depth in this chapter. It is offered as a human development tool that I have used throughout my research enabling me to maintain awareness of how I am doing at the task of being a whole human.

Biculturality

Culture is critical to the wellbeing of the human being. At the heart of the idea of bicultural socialisation is understanding that people living in a culture not developed with their interests in mind need to be socialised into two cultures: a culture of origin and the culture of residence. There are points of possible conflict and consciously attending to them protects one's inner well-being:

> To become bicultural, an individual must engage in a dual socialisation process. One acquires values, beliefs, communication and behavioural styles from a culture of origin as well as becoming exposed to the same dynamics of a majority culture. An ethnic minority will have success in becoming bicultural to the extent that crucial information and skills needed for negotiating the mainstream culture are provided, commensurate with receiving affirmation for the basic values, beliefs and behavioural styles of one's minority culture. (DeAnda, 1984)

Such socialisation allows awareness of how different cultures might conflict with one another in terms of underpinning beliefs and values so that these conflicts can be managed and worked through. Unconsciously internalised conflicts result in a lack of integration of the four dimensions of the human being. Socialisation into a culture of origin which has the individual's interests at its heart ensures that they have the inner resources to respond to external challenges presented by the culture of residence. Bicultural socialisation also works to foster ethnic identity development as an important life task. In addition, Haritatos and Benet-Martinez (2005) discuss the importance of integrating the different cultural identities we develop over time. Assessing the experience of the DoEAs against this bicultural thesis it becomes immediately apparent that we do not enjoy the benefits of bicultural socialisation as a group. As a consequence DoEAs do not engage with the ethnic identity development process as a life task. DoEAs are thus disadvantaged in British society as seen in our positioning relative to the ethnic majority as seen in Figure 6.1 (see page 118). In the typical British classroom DoSOs are afforded cultural centricity in their education whereas DoEAs are culturally decentred having no internalised positive cultural resource to sustain them. Asante (1991) defines centricity in education as:

116

... a perspective that involves locating students within the context of their own cultural references so that they can relate socially and psychologically to other cultural perspectives. Centricity is a concept that can be applied to any culture. The centrist paradigm is supported by research showing that the most productive method of teaching any student is to place his or her group within the center of the context of knowledge. For white students in America this is easy because almost all the experiences discussed in American classrooms are approached from the standpoint of white perspectives and history. American education, however, is not centric; it is Eurocentric. Consequently, non-white students are also made to see themselves and their groups as the 'acted upon'. Only rarely do they read or hear of non-white people as active participants in history.

Children from ethnic minority groups who benefit from bicultural socialisation are protected from the type of decentring that DoEAs are exposed to. Bicultural socialisation allows differentiation, something DoEAs do not benefit from, hence the problems identified in the previous chapter in my internal world. Three factors leave the black child at the whim of wider social forces: the lack of a conscious developed cultural resource designed with the interests of DoEAs at its centre; black socialisation administered by whites and the dysfunctions of an uninterrogated black culture unconsciously transmitted amongst DoEAs. As DoEAs we now have a responsibility to our young to overturn this dysfunctional and non-generative legacy that results in this black-white duality. This is where understanding what it means to be a whole human being and the significance of conscious bicultural competence come into play.

The black and white bicultural competence matrix

Embarking on the journey towards conscious bicultural competence revealed that it was most important to interrogate British culture and not African culture as many DoEAs assume. With this insight came the recognition that sustained attempts to take on African culture, a culture into which I had not been born or socialised, were doomed to failure. The belief amongst many DoEAs that British culture, the culture into which we have been socialised is not our culture is equally problematic. We neglect and ignore British culture at our peril.

The reality of the situation is that the bicultural competence matrix relates to British culture and its two subcultures: black and white as seen in Figure 8.1. Because I was in a state of psychic disorientation, confusion, social amnesia and despair I had been completely unaware that black culture had any links with British culture.

Figure 8.1: Black and White Bicultural Competence Matrix

	Unconscious	Conscious
Black and White Bicultural Incompetence	*don't know I don't know* Remedy: nurture	*know I don't know* Remedy: self-re-education
Black and White Bicultural Competence	*don't know I know* Remedy: wake from sleep Hidden and taboo knowledge	*know I know* Remedy: maintain awareness/choice social actors know but pretend they don't know

The focus of Figure 8.1 is on our awareness of black and white cultures as sub-cultures of British culture and how they shape our relationship with ourselves and one another: black and white cultures can be seen as imposter cultures which are thrown like a veil over the consciousness of two groups of people. Hidden behind these imposter cultures are various folk cultures which have been forgotten or discarded in favour of black and white cultures. For example, behind white British culture are English, Irish and Scottish cultures. In a similar vein, behind black British culture is an authentic African-Caribbean culture struggling to give life to itself. To engage with the black and white imposter cultures is to interrupt their dysfunctional outcomes on our lives. To do this we must surface the hidden and taboo knowledge relating to them on the bottom left quadrant of Figure 8.1.

To pursue this idea is to realise that black culture and, therefore, white culture, are not ethnic cultures at all. Various researchers have identified the dysfunctions in black culture. For example, McWhorter (2001) describes it as an externally imposed cultural disorder that has taken on a life of its own. Painter (1995) links black culture to the idea of soul murder. Pinderhughes (1979) describes it as a culture consisting of three elements: elements of African culture; aspects of British culture and a culture of victimhood representing the culture into which enslaved Africans were socialised during slavery. Figure 8.1 specifically focuses on black and white cultures questioning the extent to which they are understood by the DoEAs and the DoSOs who co-create and inhabit them. Without this awareness we are likely to remain trapped in the black-white duality.

Understanding the quadrants

My understanding of the matrix and the details of the quadrants of Figure 8.1 evolved as I sought to achieve transformational change using the research methods discussed in chapter one.

The unconscious bicultural incompetence quadrant

Babies enter life positioned on the quadrant of unconscious bicultural in-competence (top left quadrant of Figure 8.1) and depend on their parents and caregivers for socialisation into a design for living or culture. The quality of socialisation provided by parenting and education will have a significant impact on the consciousness of the growing child. Poor and dysfunctional socialisation can be transmitted generationally. If through their own socialisation our parents and teachers have not moved into conscious aware-ness of who they are as humans and the responsibility this entails in working consciously with culture, dysfunctions will inevitably occur. Such teachers and parents unwittingly operate as the blind leading the blind, people who perpetuate the racial inequalities between blacks and whites. This idea gives an important insight into the crucial role that education plays in the develop-ment of our children. As the child develops certain knowledge will evolve into unconscious bicultural competence and become routinised. This is neces-sary because we cannot be conscious of all things at all times. However, chil-dren mature, and as they reach the age of 12 or 13 in British culture they be-come culpable for their own actions.

With the race taboo (Thomas, 1989; Frankenberg, 1993), and therefore a culture of silence (Winton, 2003) as inherent features of British culture, our young people in the school system, in a multicultural post-colonial society, are not educated to understand how the black and white division of the world came into being much less how it continues to be perpetuated. Instead we find that most people view the world through the normalised lens of blacks, whites and different human races. Irrespective of the failures of our parents and teachers life has its own way of bringing us lessons. Depending on our responses to these lessons we either move from the top left quadrant of Figure 8.1 to the top right quadrant where we are conscious of our bicultural incompetence and engage in the process of education for critical awareness. Alternatively, we can move to the bottom left quadrant of Figure 8.1 and into a state of unconscious bicultural competence: knowing but not knowing how we know.

The unconscious bicultural competence quadrant – the quadrant of detriment

In the unconscious bicultural competence quadrant (bottom left of Figure 8.1) life experiences reveal that the binary division of the world into blacks and whites is not as natural as it is purported to be. As we journey through life we have developed a fleeting awareness of the contradictions, the social in-equality, the poverty, greed and exploitation of the many by the few. But we have become so embedded in the *status quo* that we believe we can't do any-

119

thing about it. Our moral integrity questions what we could do to change things and make the world a better place for everyone. However, other factors come into play. The fact that we are privileged by the *status quo* is perhaps sufficient reason to do nothing. Our socialisation might have left us poorly educated and lacking in self-confidence, esteem and efficacy. We might be stuck in survival mode where all we can do is to look out for our own personal interests. We might believe that we are unimportant in the world and so what we do does not matter. We have therefore learned to blame others instead of thinking about what we could be doing ourselves. Like the DoEAs we might have been stripped of our culture of origin, names, homeland and denied education and spiritual practice. We might have been dehumanised and re-created into slaves to serve the members of another group and have remained in that state of being for long centuries, struggling towards spiritual freedom.

All of us within this quadrant (Figure 8.1) would have had experiences that have made us realise that our lives are lies, that we have become spiritually destitute as we live automatic lives based on fear, repression, avoidance, denial, doubt and self-protection. We witness people in our society using different forms of anaesthesia (like alcohol and drugs) to numb themselves in all kinds of ways as a means of avoiding reality and our responsibilities as humans.

The denied and silenced issues in this quadrant of Figure 8.1 comprise the human tasks we must engage with and resolve in order to further humanity. These denied and silenced issues form the significant wall of silence and emotional turmoil that exists between blacks and whites. The majority of the problems we face in life have developed from our failure to address the issues we hide from or are hidden from us in this unconscious bicultural competence quadrant. This quadrant reminds us that we know but are unconscious of our knowing. It is the quadrant of tacit and hidden knowledge, which needs to be surfaced, understood and worked through. The reason we remain in this quadrant is because of our failures to be courageous and to live with our personal integrity intact. At every stage choices, whether for human flourishing or human degradation are being made, consciously and unconsciously, according to which quadrant of Figure 8.1 the individual occupies.

Conscious bicultural incompetence quadrant

With quality education we should move from unconscious bicultural incompetence to conscious bicultural incompetence, knowing that we don't know, realising the necessity of educating ourselves as a lifelong pursuit. If, however, we progress from unconscious bicultural incompetence to unconscious bicultural competence it is not easy to awaken from the deep sleep into which we are likely to have fallen. Becoming conscious of one's bicultural incompetence does not mean that the individual will engage with the work required to move towards conscious bicultural competence. Many people try to revert back into unconsciousness for as long as they can. The issues to be faced can feel unsurmountable. So we tell ourselves there is nothing we can do. This is how the world is. This means that there are individuals on the conscious bicultural incompetence quadrant of Figure 8.1 who are pretending to be asleep. There is an African proverb which says the most difficult person to awaken is the one who pretends to be asleep. However, for those who find themselves appalled by their unconsciousness and understand the significance of conscious bicultural incompetence, being on this quadrant is the beginning of the self-re-education process. Self-re-education is facilitated by the decision to begin to live our lives consciously, with awareness and integrity, and to face up to the self which is something most of us want to avoid. In the conscious bicultural incompetence quadrant we learn how to extend our comfort zone, take risks, as we begin learning how to act with integrity and authenticity. We know now that what we think and do matters and reaches beyond ourselves.

Conscious bicultural competence quadrant

The state of being consciously biculturally competent results in awareness and choice, but there are likely to be social actors in this quadrant of Figure 8.1: those who know but pretend they don't know. Such social actors include institutional agents with the clear agenda of maintaining the black-white duality and black subordination to whites. Being consciously biculturally competent means that we are aware of the cultures shaping our lives and their relationship with each other in terms of where and how they resonate or experience dissonance. Being consciously biculturally competent does not mean that life necessarily becomes easier or that our challenges less but that we are now equipped to meet these challenges more effectively. We know that meeting these challenges is the human task. The close relationship between conscious bicultural competence and unconscious bicultural competence should not be ignored because of the ease with which it is possible to slip from consciousness to unconsciousness.

Bicultural competence in British society

We have seen that the DoEAs and the DoSOs have been socialised for unconsciousness where race is concerned. Over the years of my research I have observed that the better educated DoSOs tend to already be aware of the findings and are in the main more surprised that I understand the issues to the extent I now do as a DoEA. Unconsciousness is not, therefore, a structural feature of white culture. This is not the case with the DoEAs. My own understanding now is that the majority of DoEAs in British society reside in the unconscious quadrants of Figure 8.1. This is in terms of culture as a phenomenon, what it means to be whole human beings and the specificities of British culture with its two subcultures. Unconsciousness for the DoEAs is the outcome of being inculturated into the British culture I have analysed and accepting the black and white experiences uncritically: a culture of privilege for those identified as whites and a culture of poverty and deprivation for those identified as blacks. Unconsciousness for DoSOs is likely to be the result of denial, unawareness, studied ignorance and of ensuring the maintenance of white privilege. To understand the black-white bicultural matrix is to begin to perceive our own dehumanisation especially in terms of how we are trapped within the invisible boundaries of the black-white duality.

Bicultural socialisation as a pre-requisite for all members of British society

It seems that bicultural socialisation must be a pre-requisite for all members of British society if we are to bring about the transformation in social justice which is required. As the DoEAs begin the process of bicultural socialisation as a means of preparing our children for entering the formal school system and wider society pressure will be placed on members of the ethnic majority to change their relationship with members of this group. This means that educators in the formal educational system will also need to be biculturally socialised. Since British culture consists of black and white subcultures we are all unconsciously socialised into one of these cultures in the context of the other. Bicultural socialisation allows us all to understand and work with the consequences of this ongoing dysfunctional differential socialisation to contradict it. Gaining understanding of the relationship between blacks, ethnic minorities and whites is also an important part of the process of developing bicultural competence. DoEAs, locked into unconsciousness, have not yet understood how ethnicity is used by other groups. For other groups, ethnicity is normalised to the extent that they have in turn become unconsciously biculturally competent.

Using the bicultural lens of analysis in this way also opens up deeper understanding of Britain's relationship with her former colonised groups and which has resulted in the white to black status continuum (Feagin, 2000) on which different ethnic minority members of the human family vie for positioning as close to the white end as possible. This shows how the rest of the human family have fallen into the trap of thinking along the lines of superior and inferior cultures as well as engaging in the drive for domination and power over others. Waking up all members of British society from the sleep of un-awareness will benefit everyone: we need to rethink the human task of developing a culture or cultures that benefit the whole human race.

Using the matrix

As an educator I use the matrix in conjunction with the five dimensional human being model introduced in chapter five with my own children, in my professional practice and the emerging British African-Caribbean com-munity to help them explore if the culture within which they live enhances their lives. It is also used as a means of facilitating people from unconscious-ness to consciousness in terms of understanding how culture shapes their lives as they move towards living as whole human beings. In the process the inhibiting features of the culture will reveal themselves as the existence of black and white cultures as subcultures of British culture did in my own case. In pursuing leads and contradictions as they occur we can piece together the jigsaw of our lives to recognise the outcomes we have unconsciously created for ourselves through our unwitting choices. The process directs us towards making new life-enhancing choices. Together, the five-dimensional human being model and the bicultural competence matrix amount to a philosophy of relating both to ourselves and other people. This process means that I can no longer look at the DoSOs as whites but I understand them as human beings who have also been damaged by the consequences of race being em-bedded in British culture. I am equally filled with compassion for members of my own group who have lived with the burden of unconsciousness for so long. These important self-reflection and developmental tools can be used by educators, parents and teachers, to focus on:

■ Our consciousness or unconsciousness of how the different cultures impacting on our lives are shaping our consciousness: congruence versus dissonance; bicultural identity integration issues

■ The basis for forming relationships with ourselves and others

■ our awareness of the human task as conscious creators of culture

■ our understanding of how black and white cultures operate as im-poster cultures and the folk cultures that are hidden behind them

■ the consequences of having conferred and foreclosed identities and cultures externally imposed on us

■ how we are doing at the task of being human – emotional and spiri-tual well-being

The process can be extended to explore any other issue such as gender to understand how it is handled within the culture. The outcome of this focus will be similar to my own experience of gaining an enhanced understanding of culture and how it connects all aspects of human experience into a whole. Consequently, although I started out with the stated intention of investigating the black experience the process has facilitated an enhanced understanding of the human experience.

Generative Educators

This chapter emphasises that we cannot avoid being cultural workers and that as parents and teachers we have a responsibility to know what it is we are transmitting through our teaching. As parents we have, as I have frequently heard Oprah Winfrey say, the most important job in the world. Teachers in the school system must be a close second. British culture with its two subcultures and my unconscious socialisation into black British culture deprived me of this awareness and resulted in the inner conflicts and frustration. This pointed me to the cause of the problems: I needed to work with the culture in which I was living to resolve my inner turmoil. It became apparent that the legacy history has left me is a re-humanising agenda beginning with myself.

Parent-educators of the DoEAs who engage in the process of bicultural socialisation will transform the life experience of other members of this group: skills will be developed for more effective engagement with the British educational system. This will have a ripple effect for teachers who are the DoSOs, forcing them to engage with their own unconscious bicultural competence where race is concerned. DoSOs who engage with the knowledge shared here towards the goal of becoming generative educators for all children have the potential to transform the education system. Thus we begin to work with the wall of silence that exists between the two groups.

9

The conscious bicultural competence
imperative for teachers

... loss of soul is a violent act, an 'unnatural' yet purposive response which
interferes with natural human vocation, evolution and elaboration, with the dignity
and elegance of imaginative expression, with the myriad, complex and simple
ways we, as human beings, have of expressing experience and making life
meaningful. This interference is an act of betrayal which results in a traumatic loss
of human dignity and response. As a modern 'condition', a wasteland results
when imagination and meaning are eradicated and existence becomes solely a
concrete and materialistic exercise, when feeling, individual thought and fantasy
become threatening and alien, invasions to be eradicated by drugs or step-by-
step how-to-fix-it manuals, and human suffering is meaningless, unattended or
encountered by a hardened, empty or dead heart. (Young, 2000)

I was angry: why should I be left with this: I didn't want it; I'd done my best for
years to reject it: I wanted no part of what was in it: the benefits of my privilege,
the restrictions, the injustice, the pain, the broken origins of the heart, the
unknown horrors. And yet it is mine: I am my father's daughter in the present,
living in a world he and my folks helped to create. (Adams, 2002)

There are other ways of being guilty of bloodshed besides stabbing with a knife,
or poisoning with a deadly drug. There is another kind of murder far less detested,
but equally black in God's sight-not the destruction of the body-but the destruction
of the soul! Not the destruction of the mere shell, the outward man, but the
murder of the real man, the inward self, the inner spirit, the soul murder which
cries for vengeance before high Heaven, concerning which we have need to offer
the prayer of David, 'Deliver me from the guilt of bloodshed, O God, The God of
my salvation. (Spurgeon, 1866)

Before we can create the world we must first unearth and destroy the myths and realities, the lies and propaganda which have been used to impress, enslave ... Facing the lies of history is a basic human responsibility. It is unpleasant to do but liberating to accomplish. It liberates us all. (Okri, 1997)

Introduction

In gaining understanding of the issues outlined so far the process itself revealed the answers to the black predicament. I had to change my mind about myself since it was unlikely that the DoSOs were going to change their mind about me. The necessity of my developing conscious bicultural competence both as a parent and an educator in the formal system became apparent. I realised that is we, the DoEAs, who must be the drivers in creating a more life-enhancing legacy for our young. In this chapter I share how I have developed my educational practice, applying my knowledge to the conflicts and challenges I experience. I briefly describe the Free Within Ourselves Academically-Based Community Service research project I have developed within the university and relate it to a discussion of the different challenges we have as educators who are caught in the oppositional relationship of the black-white duality.

The Free Within Ourselves Academically-Based Community Service Research Project

Prior to gaining the National Teaching Fellowship Scheme (NTFS) award and research fellowship in 2002 I had already spent twelve years developing my professional practice using academic research in an institutional context that adopts a colour-blind approach. Much of the research had to be carried out at the level of first-person action research/inquiry (autobiographical research) as I strove to find out what it means for me to be black and to find a fit between being black and teaching in higher education. Surfacing how I had internalised race given that it is a central British value (ONS, 2003) was crucial to this process.

I then spent years engaging experientially with knowledge as I underwent the type of re-engineering process described in chapter seven. Attempting to engage in second-person action research/inquiry with colleagues who are the DoSOs generally met with silence or disassociation. This confirmed that there was a requirement placed on me to deny my particular experiences and collude with a colour-blind approach if I am to maintain cordial relations with colleagues. Their silences left me with no choice but to use silence as data. Second person action inquiry with colleagues who are the DoEAs was not made easier by their concerns 'not to make waves' to ensure their own survival. These findings are very much in line with the literature. Despite the large numbers of DoEAs who attend the university, they have been more or less inaccessible to me because of the conscious and unconscious influence the DoSOs maintain over our lives and relationships. At the heart of our lack of association as members of a specific social category (Banton, 1997) is our perceived dependency on the DoSOs and the felt need to appease and satisfy them. Just as earlier in my career, grouping together as the DoEAs was largely understood as detrimental to our career aspirations. Consequently, students brave enough to explore their lives through the NTFS research project acknowledge how emotionally draining the experience is for them in the university.

The finding from this on-going research project substantiates much of what has been discussed in this book. Consequently, I have worked with a range of challenges including:

Lack of DoSOs support for the project

The wall of silence, denial and ignorance between DoEAs and DoSOs has meant that the support of DoSOs is not necessarily forthcoming for the project. My focus has been on empowering DoEAs to intervene in British society through developing conscious bicultural competence. This means critical engagement with British culture as opposed to our more common conforming and submissive relationship with the culture. But unsurprisingly DoSOs are not forthcoming with their support and this is perceived as a lack of permission by many DoEAs.

My commitment to the DoEAs as a group has to be high because of the new psychological contract I have agreed with myself. The paradox has surfaced that DoEAs fear our researching our own life experience because of the likely angst of the DoSOs. DoEAs do not learn about us as a group in their formal education process and there are no informal processes in place to ensure that this learning takes place systematically except perhaps in supplementary schools. As an elder in this group I am committed to working with these issues.

Fear and distrust

With poor DoSO support, fear and distrust has surrounded the research project and I have struggled to maintain my commitment to it. This demonstrates how important it is engage with the issues. No doubt my own reputation as a researcher of race works against me and therefore against the project. Because my identity has been racialised and then silenced, my developing self-knowledge is perceived as problematic.

The need for centricity in education

Centricity in education is urgently required for the DoEAs and indeed all learners in diverse classrooms. While supplementary schools have been a piecemeal means of meeting this need for the DoEAs they are no longer sufficient. The choice of adopting the centricity approach to engaging with my educational practice and life presents numerous challenges not least of which is acknowledging myself as a DoEA and what this triggers in both blacks and whites. I find myself situated between the desire for authenticity and integrity versus rejection and making the decision for authenticity.

Engaging with the DoEAs as an ethnic group

The black experience is being reframed using an ethnicity as opposed to a race lens of analysis. This challenges taken for granted assumptions about blacks, allows us to work with issues of relating to our lack of unity, cohesiveness and community infrastructure as a group. It also begins to dismantle the black-white duality.

Application of knowledge to the life experiences of DoEAs

In supporting the idea of centricity the project also supports the application of knowledge to the life experiences of the DoEAs. Such knowledge is relevant to both the DoEAs and the DoSOs in crystallising the ongoing impact of slavery in the 21st century and why and how it continues to be a growing industry (Bales, 1999).

Ending collusion with the race taboo

Presenting myself unashamedly as a BAC woman whose challenge is to work through the black and white experiences and identities is also a daunting experience because we have all been socialised to observe the race taboo and to expect blacks to be inferior to whites. Students either feel liberated or uncomfortable about my acknowledgement of difference as their teacher. My experience has shown that acknowledging and working with the history of slavery has the potential for us to become free within ourselves. Dewey (1934) acknowledged that this is the purpose of education. Issues of history and culture also need to be worked with to enable the identity formation process: this is evident in terms of the impact they have on the inner experience of both the DoEAs and DoSOs.

Developing a human-centred teaching and learning approach

The project uses the human-centred passionate appreciation approach which has evolved throughout its life (Gordon, 2005) and advocates centricity for all learners. This is because the focus is on achieving a revolution of the self as seen in chapter seven.

These challenges have been taken on in the context of the knowledge being developed in working towards competence, mutuality and making myself integral to British society. The scale of the work involved made us, as the DoEAs participating in the project, realise the need for a research centre.

The Centre for British African-Caribbean Studies

Through the process of this longitudinal research I had been creating a margin of space (Elkins, 1968) in my own mind-world and was now, with the project, creating a physical one in the institution. I had come to the realisation that I had a valuable contribution that matters to make and that I had met the two criteria identified by Elkins (1968) as necessary to resisting slavery. Working with DoEAs on the project, students in the university and the community outreach route of the project confirmed the usefulness of my work and the necessity for a research centre within the higher education context to focus on the BAC experience. The role of this centre is to foster understanding of their respective experiences for both the DoEAs and the DoSOs. The Centre is based on the premise that knowledge of one's own history and culture is essential to learning how to relate to people of other groupings. This is because the task of building genuine and authentic relationships across differences is crucial to the future well-being of British society. Because of the unique and fixed nature of the relationship between the DoEAs and the DoSOs, which has largely been silenced, this task presents a threat to the racial *status quo*. In meeting the challenges of this perceived threat the need for a further project through which the experience of undergoing a metanoia could be shared revealed itself.

The *Metanoia* Project[2007-2034]

The processes I have undergone on my own research journey amount to a *metanoia*. The term '*metanoia*' has a Greek root and means a change of mind or heart. The *Metanoia* Project[2007-2034] (TMP) aims to facilitate a change of mind or heart in the DoEAs and the DoSOs achieved through understanding and working with our shared history as blacks and whites under British culture. TMP is visionary and looks to a time when the DoEAs and the DoSOs are no longer looking across the centuries at one another in pain, bitterness, resentment, distrust and fear. TMP's purpose is to make concerted, strategic and focused efforts during the 25 years between 2007, the 200th anniversary of the abolition of the slave trade, and 2034, the 200th anniversary of the abolition of slavery itself, to make a breakthrough in surfacing and resolving the crucial issues. This includes the psychological, emotional and spiritual slavery in which many remain trapped.

TMP understands teachers as servants of civilisation who have an important role to play in the project of furthering humanity. The primary aim of TMP is to facilitate all teachers, formal and informal, to develop conscious bicultural competence as a key component of their training and continuous professional development. It focuses on the interrelated and mutually reinforcing core capacities for change:

- personal vision building (to go within and take a stand for a preferred future)

- inquiry (internalising norms, habits and techniques for continuous learning)

- mastery (behaving our ways into new visions and ideas) and

- collaboration (route to organisational/societal change (Fullan, 1993).

TMP has also evolved to adopt what Palmer (1992) calls a movement approach to change where the DoEAs and DoSOs are 'divided no more', opting instead for the rehumanised condition shown in chapter seven. Palmer identifies four stages in a movement:

- Isolated individuals decide to stop leading divided lives

- These people discover each other and form groups for mutual support

- Empowered by community they learn to translate private problems into public concerns

- Alternative rewards emerge to sustain the movement's vision which may force the conventional reward system to change

In Palmer's view courage is stimulated by the understanding that our unconscious collaboration with external forces crushes the spirit and with this realisation comes anger: no punishment can possibly be more severe than the punishment that comes from conspiring in the denial of one's own integrity. The purpose of stage two is to wrap the individual's inner decision in a resolve that can only come from being heard by a supportive community. Such groups help people to discover that their problems are not private but have been caused by public conditions and require public remedies. In the fourth stage the movement intersects with organisations and the broader social system.

The desired outcome of TMP(teach) is for teachers who understand themselves culturally and who are equipped for working with the issues discussed. The primary obstacle to this occurring is our embeddedness as blacks and whites in a dysfunctional culture which has silence at its heart (Winton, 2003) and conflict avoidance (Dhreuv, 1992) as behaviours that are transmitted generationally within the two groups. Silence and conflict avoidance work effectively to stifle our ability to work with the human task of being conscious creators of culture. This book paves the way for this by violating the silence that surrounds race as an issue as well as presenting the underlying conflict in a way which reveals a way forward using the bicultural competence matrix. This involves waking people up to what it means to be whole human beings starting with ourselves as teachers and parents. In acknowledging black culture as an inherent component of British culture it becomes a British cultural issue to be worked through as opposed to an ethnic minority issue for the smaller collective to work with amongst its own membership. This is the significance of the Centre for British African-Caribbean Studies (CBACS) being housed in the higher education setting.

A first step towards furthering humanity is in acknowledging blacks as the DoEAs and whites as the DoSOs. This challenges the practices of the institution of social interaction as well as surfacing the underlying issues, visible and invisible legacies of slavery, we block and repress.

Although this chapter speaks to all teachers, teachers who are the DoEAs are the crucial catalysts for change. The task facing DoEAs is not about seeking to change others while we remain the same but about changing ourselves to be the change we want to see.

Professional ethics

Korman (cited by Midgette and Meggert (1991)) suggests we have no choice but to participate in TMP, noting:

> ... the provision of professional services to persons of culturally diverse backgrounds by persons not competent in understanding and providing professional services to such groups shall be considered unethical; that it shall be equally unethical to deny such persons professional services because the present staff is inadequately prepared; that it shall be the obligation of all service agencies to employ competent persons or to provide continuing education for the present staff to meet the service needs of the culturally diverse population it serves.

This idea is supported by Fullan's (1993) call for teachers to combine the moral foundation of teaching with the skills of a change agent because 'teaching at its core is a moral profession'. To achieve this he points us to the four key capacities identified above. Dhruev (1992) makes a similar link between personal action and institutional counterparts in acknowledging black professionals as 'social pioneers'.

Many of us fail to take on the challenges presented to us in life by choosing instead to avoid them, as seen in Figure 8.1 on the unconscious bicultural competence quadrant. Reflecting on these ideas is important for those of us who are teachers. Educating with the aim of developing a new psychological contract amongst DoEAs as a group and between the DoEAs and the DoSOs will make an important contribution to British society and intra- and inter-group relationships. As teachers we are enhancers of human life as opposed to the soul murderers who are described in the opening quotes to this chapter. This is especially pertinent because of the nature of institutionalised racism in Britain (Macpherson, 1999) and how it works as black socialisation. Korman (cited by Midgette and Meggert (1991) identifies a number of challenges for us:

- recognising, accepting and valuing the cultural differences in our nation

- searching for historical truths by the university and students alike

- using research to explicate cultural understanding

- adopting more democratic attitudes and values

- adopting a clarified philosophical position on pluralism

- adopting a process conceptualisation of multicultural/antiracist education

- developing the ability to view society from diverse ethnic perspectives

- developing knowledge of the emerging styles of ethnicity and its teaching implications

In taking on these challenges we counteract key cultural patterns which may have served their purpose in the past but have now become dysfunctional. These include working with silence and developing the ability to negotiate conflict for human development if we are to intervene more effectively with the workings of the black-white duality in the education system.

Silence

The critical quadrant of Figure 8.1, where most of our problems lie is that of unconscious bicultural competence – the quadrant of denial, avoidance, fear, ignorance, distrust, anger, resentment, silence and all the other negative emotions that assail human beings. We need to engage with the human task on a daily moment by moment basis as whole human beings, role modelling this way of being to our students. To live like this we need to develop the ability to negotiate conflict and find the courage to interrupt the social distance mechanisms revealed in chapter six. We cannot continue to act collusively and in complicity with the silence and denial that supports social inequality between the DoEAs and the DoSOs.

Teachers who practice silence, as a response to race, place the burden of race squarely on the shoulders of the children whose character they are responsible for moulding in the classroom. Holdt's (1997) idea that 85 per cent of the emotional energy of the child whose identity has been foreclosed as black is tied up in managing race as an issue so as to protect the emotional responses of their teachers is a significant one. If true, it should stop us in our tracks. What is increasingly clear is that the negativity of the life experiences of the DoEAs is a result of the failures of the DoEAs and the DoSOs as adults (especially teachers) in working with the black-white duality and the dysfunctions it embodies. Teacher training programmes that inadequately prepare teachers for engaging with these issues leave those teachers with a colourblind position intact.

Conscious bicultural competence allows teachers to enter the classroom able to explore issues of race and culture with their learners. Accordingly, development of conscious bicultural competence should be part of all teacher training programmes in post-colonial societies so that teachers work with the historical legacies of slavery and colonisation. The education system is the ideal context within which to begin the process of consciously working with British culture to create a more human centred life enhancing culture.

Learning to negotiate conflict for human development

In our post-colonial multicultural society conflict is an everyday likelihood. Although the automatic responses of silence, evasiveness and defensiveness are not working, we generally persist with them. Dhruev (1992) maintains that the negotiation of conflict is essential for the development of the individual, family, community or nation. He cites Freud and Minuchin to make his point:

> The disagreement is between the external world and the id, and it is because the ego, loyal to its inmost nature, takes sides with the external world that it becomes in conflict with the id. But please observe that what creates the determination for the illness is not the fact of this conflict – for disagreements of this kind between reality and the id are unavoidable and it is one of the ego's standing tasks to mediate in them ... (Freud, 1986)

> There are many phases in a family's own natural evolution that require negotiation of new family rules ... in this process, conflicts inevitably arise. Ideally, the conflicts

will be resolved by negotiations of transition, and the family will adapt successfully. These conflicts offer an opportunity for growth by all family members. (Minuchin, 1974)

Conflict avoidance behaviours are dysfunctional. Both the DoEAs and the DoSOs need to work with the largely silenced and unacknowledged historical conflict that exists between the two groups to move beyond the *status quo*. The courage we need is for doing what is ethically right not only for ourselves and our group but for all humanity. This especially applies to me, as a DoEA, and a British citizen. I am a person who has been given the theoretical rights of freedom in British society but not equipped with the tools to claim this freedom (see Beals and Spindler, 1973).

The black-white duality in the education system
The literature on the experience of black children in the education system suggests a number of reasons for their underachievement, none of which acknowledges the silenced relationship between the DoEAs and the DoSOs and how it works to maintain social inequality. For example, since the arrival of the DoEAs from the Caribbean in the 1950s various government initiatives have been taken with the stated aim of overcoming the challenges these children face in the British school system. With the historical relationship silenced these children are problematised. So, despite how long the DoEAs have been in Britain little has changed. In 1987 Gurnah accused the government of containing public opinion by 'placating, reassuring, diffusing, confusing, legitimising, manipulating it and saving public money' through setting up committees so that the initial grievance has been depoliticised by the time they've completed their deliberations. He accused the government of using the 'containment' strategy of social distancing even at some expense.

In 2003 the DFES *Aiming Higher* report acknowledged the need to develop in all teachers the confidence and skills to manage diverse classrooms and respond positively and effectively to different groups. The report especially mentioned the need to offer teachers guidance on managing the anticipated conflict in schools over issues faced by African Caribbean children. Here is the black-white duality at work. The report makes no mention of the need for teachers to understand themselves culturally so they can understand the source of the anticipated conflict. But the London Development Agency's (LDA, 2004:10) research does identify teacher attitude towards black boys as producing negative outcomes, stating:

> At the heart of the school agenda for change must be improved pupil teacher relationships for pupils from African-Caribbean backgrounds. Everything else flows

from this – high expectations, positive teacher attention, encouragement and support. Addressing issues of emotional intelligence and racial stereotyping is far
harder than making pedagogical adaptations. It will take profound levels of reflection, integrity and courage for the shifts that are so urgently needed to take place.

Reading between the lines of this statement it appears that the LDA is calling
teachers to engage with the history discussed in chapter four. The focus on
teachers addressing issues of emotional intelligence, profound levels of
reflection, integrity and courage implicitly acknowledges the work required
on the unconscious bicultural competence quadrant of Figure 8.1. This is because both the DoEAs and the DoSOs have been unconsciously socialised
into the black and white oppositional cultures that make up British culture
and are more than likely to have internalised the conflict in their inner world
(Davidson, 2001). Consequently teachers need to be consciously biculturally
competent.

The goal: bicultural identity integration and transformation

Biculturalism is concerned with the inner experience of culture, including
points of possible conflict and its impact on the individual, the group and
their wellbeing. Biculturalism and multiculturalism are mutually exclusive
ideas: biculturalism is about taking care of our inner world whereas multiculturalism is a way of looking at and managing the external world. For us
teachers to support students effectively in the process of bicultural identity
integration and transformation we must have worked with these issues for
ourselves. This will help to transform the dysfunctions of the black-white
duality in which both the DoEAs and the DoSOs participate.

It was the unconscious inner rejection of my own cultural inheritances, as
dictated by British culture, which threw me into crisis. I was alienated from
British culture because of its rejection of me; unconsciously I refused to
identify with African culture because of its stigmatisation in British culture
and I was ashamed of my slavery background, as seen in the Caribbean culture. These inheritances were juxtaposed against English white culture, within which I lived as a subordinated member of the group. The conflicting
values I internalised as a result of all this left me in turmoil and bicultural dissonance. Although Erikson (1950) acknowledges that perfection of the
developmental process is rarely achieved, nevertheless the objective is to
acquire needed sources of strength to deal with the contested terrain between
somatic development and social circumstances. He argues for demonstrating
competence, working out sensible ways of becoming integral to a community
and carrying through on a commitment to mutuality (Hoover *et al*, 1997) as I
have been learning to do.

The oppositional relationship that exists between Africa and Britain had existed in my psyche. The denial, the blocking out of the inhumane treatment of enslaved Africans in the Caribbean and of the DoEAs in the white British psyche had also taken place in my own mind-world. The critical task in terms of becoming consciously biculturally competent is in understanding and combining these three cultural components into an integrated whole in my own psychological world.

All members of the society, and indeed a globalising world, need to undergo a similar identity integration and transformation process. More specifically, we teachers should also be working with the unique nature of the bicultural challenge faced by the DoEAs and the DoSOs. For the DoEAs the challenge is one of bicultural identity formation and integration at two levels: first, at the level of the oppositional black and white cultures which they have unconsciously detrimentally internalised because of their mono-cultural socialisation and second, at the level of British and African cultures.

For the DoSOs the challenge is to form a bicultural identity in terms of understanding black and white cultures as distinct from their culture of origin. Teachers who have not worked through these issues in their own lives will not be in a position to facilitate this learning but are likely to unconsciously perpetuate the black-white duality. The *Metanoia* Project acknowledges that different challenges are presented to the DoEAs and the DoSOs. These are considered in the next sections.

Teachers who are the descendants of enslaved Africans

The Mayor of London identifies black teachers as giving black pupils more effective care and this is supported by Palmer (1993):

> There are reasons to care about teaching that are rooted deep in the human soul. Teaching is simply another word for the ancient and elemental bond that exists between the elders of a tribe and their young. When the bond is broken, both groups feel fearful and incomplete, and both will wish to reweave the relationship, no matter how profoundly alienated they may be.

A particular responsibility is laid on teachers who are the DoEAs to participate in The *Metanoia* Project to develop our conscious bicultural competence so that we can intervene more effectively in British society. Cummins (1986) has noted that widespread school failure does not occur in minority groups that are positively oriented towards their own and the dominant culture, that do not perceive themselves as inferior to the dominant group and that are not alienated from their own cultural values. Cummins' view augments my desire for an end to the black-white duality. This insight points to the necessity of teachers who are the DoEAs to take up leadership roles in British society via their own ethnic group. They are the elders of the DoEAs and have a responsibility to their young. We have responsibilities to our young that demand our engagement as active citizens with British culture.

In his introduction to the 2003 LDA report the Mayor of London declares that black parents and black teachers must take on the personal responsibility '...even in the face of resistance' for their children's learning. This means learning how to negotiate conflict and this demands a confident sense of our own humanity. Relating the idea of negotiating conflict to the teaching and learning context is important. Simon (1992) guides us towards the notion of remembrance, the practice by which certain images and stories of a collective past were brought together with a person's feelings and comprehension of their embodied presence in time and space. He inspired me to think about working towards the time when I could engage with learners at the level of the stories and images of the past which live on and affect us in the present and in our relationships with one another, even in the classroom. Simon shared his vision of a pedagogy of possibility that does not require the obliteration of the past and its replacement with a new truth. He argues for a fundamental reconfiguration and rereading of the documents of tradition in a way that might help 'reveal the present as a revolutionary moment' in the classroom in interactions between teacher and student and *vice versa*. I have been particularly moved by Simon's thought that:

> There is a secret agreement between past generations and the present one. Our coming was expected on earth. Like every generation that preceded us, we have been endowed with a weak messianic power, a power to which the past has a claim. (Simon, 1992:147)

I have come to understand why the DoEAs are in Britain in the 21st century. C L R James (1984) urged DoEAs to remove their focus from the past history of slavery and look instead to the future history of slavery. As the DoEAs we have entered British society marked by our location within larger systems of power and privilege that have shaped our experiences, but we teachers are also social activists. It is in the politics of our practice that the ethical question posed earlier is answered.

Becoming British African Caribbean in the institutional context

Engaging in the process of becoming a whole human being in the institutional context has been an important component of my research journey. I have chosen to work with cultural forces instead of running away from them, although I have been tempted to. Working with British culture has been important because:

- it has enabled me to be an effective role model in the classroom, contradicting the claim that black children do not have role models

- it has been important in role modelling to all groups a non-stereotypical perception of what it means to be a DoEA

- I can put forward a view of life as process with the transformational and self-renewal processes at work

- I can illustrate how to challenge the view of culture as something that is fixed

Aspects of the process of becoming BAC by grasping clearly how my consciousness was shaped by British culture were explained in chapter seven. Palmer (1997) aids understanding of how identity and integrity come together in our classroom practice when he says they have 'as much to do with our shadows and limits, our wounds and fears, as with our strengths and potentials'. Identity understood in this sense is a moving intersection of the inner and outer forces that make us who we are '… converging in the irreducible mystery of being human'. Integrity is the choice for wholeness which means becoming more real by acknowledging the whole of who we are. In my own case acceptance of myself as a DoEA born into black culture, an externally imposed cultural disorder, has been critical to this wholeness.

As a black teacher in a white university my credibility is clearly on the line given the underlying dynamics that frame the ongoing black and white relationship. How do we represent and present ourselves in the classroom and education system? Using my own experience as I journey towards conscious bicultural competence I seek a cultural form that is reflective of who I am as a whole human being. Trying to return to a mythical romanticised African culture, as many DoEAs do, is not appropriate to my needs that are now about authenticity, integrity and transformation. Cultures cannot be bought ready made off the shelf. Instead, I draw on the cultural experiences that inform my life. Pinderhughes (1979) model of black culture consists of three dimensions: residues of African culture; black culture as seen in a culture of victimisation, poverty, deprivation and soul murder and aspects of white English culture. In addition to these three dimensions there is also the British-English African-Caribbean dimension which is representative of the emergent authentic and creative strivings of a group of DoEAs as we work with what history and circumstances has given us to create something new and different for ourselves and our progeny.

My life task necessarily is to understand these different dimensions of cultural socialisation through surfacing what I have been living unconsciously so that choices can be made about what to keep and what to discard. The erroneous belief systems introduced through slavery and colonisation and which have been consistently transmitted over centuries are being discarded. The outcome of this process is represented in Figure 9.1.

Figure 9.1: British African-Caribbean Bicultural Competence Matrix

	Unconscious	Conscious
British-English and African Bicultural Incompetence	*don't know I don't know* Remedy: nurturing	*know I don't know* Remedy: self-re-education
British-English and African Bicultural Competence	*don't know I know* Remedy: needs waking from sleep	*know I know* Remedy: maintain awareness/choice

I am now in the top right quadrant engaged in a process of self-re-education. As an elder of this group I am now in a position to facilitate and mentor those at the earlier stages of the BAC life-cycle in terms of nurturing appropriate to the needs of our members living in British society. In this sense a cultural form is being developed that is designed to protect the interests of the DoEAs as a group for the first time in our history since our recreation in the 16th century. This is the quadrant on which we need teachers who are BACs and on which we are capable of taking on the challenges presented by the Mayor of London. On the conscious bicultural incompetence quadrant we are aware of the workings of black and white cultures and their dehumanising outcomes.

As BACs we are committed to evolving a folk culture that reflects our own authentic and creative strivings in the world and which we engage in transmitting to future generations. As I now work with culture I find myself in the midst of an exciting process of determining how I want to be in the world. I am looking back over my life noticing the tracks left by history for the first time. The folk culture being designed is representative of the cultural experiences identified earlier. The dominant culture is no longer black British culture but the BAC cultural form which is acknowledged as the authentic and creative strivings of the members of this group. Within this BAC culture and identity signs are to be found of our purpose for being as a group. This cultural form extends back in time reweaving our relationship with Africa. BAC culture is being derived from our own inner experience, as well as the culture of our ancestors, as we engage with our own life-worlds, extending outwards in numerous ways into the external world of other people's lives. This conforms to MacTaggart's (2004) acknowledgement that people have always drawn on a variety of sources to define and express themselves, for example as Scottish and British, Jewish and British or Muslim, Pakistani and British. Acknowledging the British, African and Caribbean cultures that have influenced us allow us to draw on a variety of sources to define and express ourselves.

Teachers who are the descendants of slave-owners

It becomes apparent that the DoSOs also need to unravel the cultural influences that impact on their lives, shaping their inner culture and relationship to other people. This is not just something minority teachers need to do. These teachers need also to engage in the form of cultural work described throughout so that they can take responsibility for the culture they are transmitting. Many DoSOs deny racism. This book has not focussed on race and racism but on historical legacies, visible and invisible, as a means of developing understanding of how we are complicit in maintaining social inequality beyond our conscious awareness. DoSOs who are teachers must engage with assumptions relating to race that underpin the culture. Such work should be understood as taking care of their spiritual, mental and emotional hygiene.

In earlier chapters I have shown how the DoSOs often unwittingly become active agents in protecting white interests as they administer black socialisation, otherwise termed racism, on behalf of British culture. Richardson (2003) writes of learning about a history '... that I had not known or understood ... that my education had hidden. I was stunned. And I was, quite frankly, angry that my education had left me ignorant of so much that I needed to know in order to understand my own life'. I am also familiar with DoSOs who reject British and white identifiers acknowledging themselves instead as English or Irish. My experience has shown that surfacing the reasons for the denial of these cultural influences to be important. DoSOs need to understand the necessity of owning white culture and therefore British culture as I had to learn to own black culture as the culture into which I was born and which has shaped me. Acknowledgement instead of denial helped me to understand the need to work with black culture in the ways I am now doing. DoSOs who do this will not be doing this for the DoEAs but most importantly for themselves – learning about what it means to be white. This means learning that they have also had an externally imposed cultural disorder placed over their lives and within which they are living unconsciously. Richardson (2003) argues this is essential in understanding that whiteness is both an advantage and a disadvantage. It is a disadvantage because the DoSOs have no idea that they live with white privilege. Instead they believe that they are treated with respect because they are valuable in themselves.

Becoming British-English in the institutional context

It is also important for teachers who are the DoSOs to role model the process of becoming whole human beings as an integral part of the inquiry process in the classroom. The reasons for this include enlightened self-interest without which, Richardson (2003) argues, 'our education, our social institutions, our communities, our humanity continues to be tarnished and diminished'. Another reason is for their children and so that they can see a generation of DoSOs who truly understand justice, who live with one another with respect and solidarity. The final reason offered by Richardson is that of '... our own integrity. How can we be silent in the face of the devastating effect of racism and maintain our sense of integrity?' DoSOs have societal power and need to take responsibility for how this power is used consciously or unconsciously. How power is wielded over the life-chances of the DoEAs and other non-white people is important. Asking teachers who are the DoSOs to risk looking at themselves as racialised beings is to ask them to violate the silence which keeps superiorised white and inferiorised black identities in place.

Like myself the DoSOs who have been socialised into white British culture and can trace their ancestry back to the English are likely to have conflicting identities. Their matrix would look as follows:

Figure 9.2: British-English Bicultural Competence Matrix

	Unconscious	Conscious
British and English Bicultural Incompetence	*don't know I don't know* Remedy: nurturing	*know I don't know* Remedy: self-re-education
British and English Bicultural Competence	*don't know I know* Remedy: needs waking from sleep	*know I know* Remedy: maintain awareness/choice

As in the case of the DoEAs, teachers who are the DoSOs, need to be facilitated to reach the top right hand quadrant and acquire the capabilities to lead change on these issues. These teachers will acknowledge their socialisation into white British culture resulting in a commitment to transform it. They will take on board their culture of origin and begin to engage in the same type of cultural recreation as the DoEAs.

This is necessarily so since the black-white bicultural matrix acknowledges white culture as an externally imposed cultural disorder. For on-lookers of the white experience studying 'whiteness' offers important insights into the experience. Whiteness originated in seventeenth-century English Atlantic colonies as a marker for who could own African slaves. To gain the privileges of racism many non-English-speaking European ethnic groups gave up their languages and ethnic traditions by melting into the dominant Anglo culture and absorbing the prevalent racist beliefs (Gossett, 1963; Ignatiev, 1995; Brodkin, 1998). All those who identified as white became naturalised descendants: they gave up their ethnic identity in order to partake of the privileges of whiteness passed on by slave owners.

If the vast majority of white people whose cultures have been actively repressed and marginalised were to reclaim their own folk culture there would be no need for them to appropriate other people's. Whites appropriate because they are looking for something deeply important that has been stolen from them and they cannot find it within the bounds of whiteness. In just the same way I couldn't find what I was looking for within the bounds of blackness. As a result we seek what we are looking for outside. Jenson (2005) acknowledges four types of fear that white people live with.

- the fear of facing the fact that some of what DoSOs have is unearned
- the fear of losing what the DoSOs have if the economic, political and social systems become more just and equitable
- fear of non-white people gaining the kind of power over whites which whites have monopolised over the DoEAs
- the fear of being seen and seen-through by non-white people in terms of the racism that most whites carry in their hearts and minds despite claims of anti-racism

Howard (1999:22) gives important insights into this phenomenon when he shares how at Stonehenge he penetrated the 'fence' (of white culture) that separated him from his own English folk culture – the culture of his ancestors:

> This was a magic night for me. I felt the presence of the ancient Celts who had chanted here their prayers to earth and sky; performing their rituals through the secret geometry of these same stones. The circle was drawn, and we were inside the space created for us, the place designed to teach us about ourselves, our relationship to each other and our connection to everything else outside the ring of stone. This is the function of culture – to provide a context, a circle of meaning and a sense of relationship to all life.

Lawson (2003) writes about the hidden wounds that the DoSOs hide within themselves while Hitchcock (2001) writes about the DoSOs as racial beings pointing to the need for a metamorphosis. These ideas confirm my own understanding of white culture also being an externally imposed cultural disorder but one which many whites seem to have been happy to take on and to perpetuate. Alcoff's (1998) paper on white people's attempts to move towards a proactive position against racism also makes interesting reading and a valuable contribution to this discussion. The book 'How the Irish became white' (Ignatiev, 1995) also gives important insights into the historical process.

Generative Educators

The *Metanoia* Project[2007-2034] presents educators who are the DoEAs and the DoSOs with the challenge of working through the issues raised in this book where the black-white duality is concerned. Acknowledging our true relationship as DoEAs and DoSOs living with unresolved visible and invisible legacies must now be done as we work through the silence, avoidance and denial that have underpinned our relationship for so long. Understanding that black children are seen as problem children because of our failures as adults should mean something significant to all of us. Engaging with the human task of attending to these historical legacies will result in each one of us realising that we are important, can make a difference and have a contribution to make. The process is likely to be particularly challenging for us as the DoEAs. However, as we work to bring together identity and integrity in our classrooms we will experience a *metanoia*. Ending black and white socialisation requires us to change our systems, institutions and churches as well as ourselves. It cannot be done by merely reducing prejudice and learning to get along better, leaving the systems and institutions intact leaves the problem of race intact.

In a place of conscious bicultural incompetence as teachers we take on the responsibility as servants of civilisation in wrestling with culture instead of living with what has been passed down as if it is fixed and complete despite the obvious dysfunctions. As BACs we are critical to interrupting the current *status quo*. Not least of these responsibilities is to work with our own human status (see chapter five) and the defensive routines (see chapter six) which work to inhibit individual and organisational learning and prevent us from taking advantage of multiple perspectives. In the next chapter focus is placed on the DoEAs as a group and the work that needs to be done now to provide the support base, margin of space and, therefore, symbolic and physical home for its members as we move towards becoming a people of destiny.

10

Clipped wings can fly again

... ethnic communities plan, influence and need culturally relevant services and activities at various levels, and use official data as one source of knowledge about themselves. Their wish to distinguish themselves provides a strong basis for establishing classifications such as this. (ONS, 2003)

... The pressures in Jamaica were not simply the pressure of race or those of poverty. They were the accumulated pressures of the slave society, the colonial society, the underdeveloped, overpopulated, agricultural country; and they were beyond the control of any one 'leader'. The situation required not a leader, but a society which understood itself and had purpose and direction.
(Naipaul, 2002)

There is no such thing as a powerless people. There are only those who have not seen and have not used their power and will. It would seem a miraculous feat, but it is possible for the unvalued ones to help create a beautiful new era in human history. New vision should come from those who suffer most and who love life the most. The marvellous responsibility of the unheard and the unseen resides in this paradox. Nature and history are not just about the survival of the fittest, but also about the survival of the wisest, the most adaptive and the most aware.
(Okri, 1997:103)

For too long we have been dreaming a dream from which we are now waking up; the dream that if we just improve the socioeconomic situations of people, everything will be okay, people will become happy. The truth is that as the struggle for survival has subsided, the question has emerged: survival for what? Ever more people today have the means to live, but no meaning to live for.
(Viktor Frankl cited in Krasko, 1997)

Introduction

Many DoEAs believe that the black experience in the world can only be changed by those who created it in the first place: the English/ Europeans. My research journey has shown that we can change our minds about ourselves, our life, the world and our experience will change accordingly. The problems faced by the DoEAs seem not as dire and intractable as previously believed. Issues, such as DuBois' (1903) double consciousness, highlighted for decades, has now been crystallised in an individually and group relevant way allowing us to begin to address them. The ideas, strategies and tools shared throughout are the first steps in taking back control of our own lives and ending the dysfunctional relationship we have maintained with the British-English for centuries.

Jacob Holdt (1997) provides powerful insights into how white perception of blacks result in our failing and, therefore, why differentiation is so important to our well-being:

> ... black and white children enter pretty much on the same level in first grade in the school system. On the average whites make it in ... a straight line up to college. But black American children start getting affected by internalized racism – believing our negative thinking of them – very early. And after 4th grade it starts showing – they start distrusting themselves, doubt their own futures and gradually loose their motivation – and therefore they start falling behind in the school system. They turn inattentive, turn off and often become hostile the more they lose hope. That lack of hope is so devastating. If you have no hope, there is no way you are ever going to make it. So after 4th grade they fall behind whites. And then this become a self-increasing process, they fall further and further behind the whites and immigrants. And by the time they should make it into college – not to speak of Ivy League schools – they are so far behind that there is no way the great majority of them can get accepted. They have long ago learned to live with the street and therefore end up in greater numbers in prison than in college.

The insight gained from this extract, when considered with the parallels that can be drawn from this research, is sufficient incentive for us as the DoEAs to wake up out of the sleep of unconsciousness and take responsibility for the education and future of our children. It also points to the necessity of working with the culture within which we live as opposed to looking outside it to find solutions to our problems. Everything shared in the previous chapter in relation to teachers applies to the DoEAs. We also have important work to do on and for ourselves.

The *Metanoia* Project (bac)

The *Metanoia* Project(bac)[2007-2034] with its focus on the British African-Caribbean community complements The *Metanoia* Project(teach) for educators by focussing on supporting DoEAs to make the transition from blacks to BACs. In chapter nine important challenges were presented to teachers who are the DoEAs. TMP(bac) seeks to support these teachers – elders – through working with the DoEAs as a group to develop a functional community with the aim of facilitating an achieved identity. TMP(bac) amounts to a social movement amongst the DoEAs, complementary to that for teachers, aimed at ending the black-white duality. Key tasks of the TMP(bac) include:

- Developing a collective will to thrive amongst the DoEAs as a group through developing a new psychological contract with ourselves and our generations

- Embracing the legacy of slavery

- Developing conscious bicultural competence (re-education) and in the process working out sensible ways of becoming integral to British society and identifying as British while carrying through a commitment to mutuality.

The rest of the chapter explores these tasks in more depth.

Developing a collective will to thrive in our own right as a distinctive group

The development of a collective will to thrive in our own right as a distinctive ethnic group is critical to an agenda for transformational change for British African-Caribbeans (BAC). Attempts have been made over the years (Giles, 1977) but without the insights contained in this book. This is because most analysis of the black experience is carried out within the boundaries and limitations of the black-white duality whereas I have adopted a transcendental approach to culture. The act of developing a collective will to thrive in our own right removes us from the margins of British society as shown in Figure 10.1, overleaf. It also gives us the opportunity to develop a life-enhancing culture of our own. In so doing we remove our focus from the DoSOs and place it on ourselves. We can then provide our young with the collective support (culture) that is now lacking for them as a group in British society. They will have advocates in the form of the senior adults and elders in their group. They will no longer be left unsupported vulnerable to social forces.

The critical point about ethnic groups that DoEAs must understand is that ethnicity provides a physical and symbolic home, a place of belonging for groups of people. New babies are born into these groups and as they grow develop a sense of pride in this symbolic home and their people, enabling them to say to the world: this is where I belong, these are the people who care for me, this is the place where I return when I have lost my way, when I want to be nurtured and cared for. Black culture does not provide this symbolic haven of belonging, homeliness and support and was not designed to do so. Consequently, babies born into black culture are handed over to the DoSOs – our recreators. Developing the collective will to not just survive but thrive through creating such a haven for our members is an imperative if we are to take the necessary steps of breaking out of the black-white duality identified in chapter seven as dominating the inner culture of the DoEAs. Developing such a collective will, through identifying as BACs instead of blacks, enables us to have a positive cultural legacy, as opposed to an externally imposed cultural disorder, to pass on to our offspring. In this way we begin the process of ending the generational transmission of a culture of deprivation, poverty, victimhood and soul murder.

In addition, making the decision to study the world from the location of a British African-Caribbean (see Figure 10.1 below) gives a different vantage point from which we can witness the black-white duality at work and in a way that is not possible when trapped within it. Inside the black-white duality we are trapped within the unconscious bicultural competence quadrant, surviving as opposed to living.

Figure 10.1: Adopting the British African-Caribbean Perspective

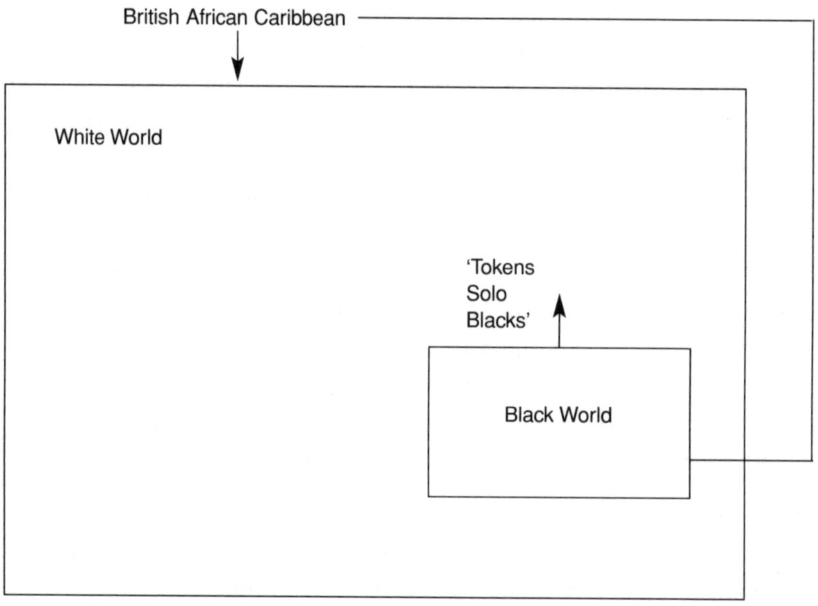

This is because the conferred black identity which British culture socialises us into, in the midst of white culture, imprisons us in the psychic prison of race caught up in a dysfunctional symbiotic and dependant relationship with the DoSOs. In this psychic prison we live in a state of anger, resentment and blame as blacks relative to whites whether internalised as in my case or externalised, as in the case of those DoEAs regarded as aggressive.

In multicultural societies governments govern through communities with the onus on the communities to approach government for the support they need (Phillips and Berman, 2003) and this has been lost to us as blacks. Instead, undifferentiated from the ethnic majority because of the black-white duality we continue in a dysfunctional subordinated relationship to them. This insight has not been lost to the host of ethnic minority groups residing in the UK who have an alternative cultural perspective from which to view British culture. It has not been the DoSOs *per se* who have prevented the DoEAs being free within ourselves, as is generally assumed but an outcome of the black-white duality working silently via British culture causing the DoEAs to unconsciously give away our personal power to the DoSOs. In this way the DoEAs, wittingly and unwittingly have allowed the current situation to evolve thus far for ourselves and our progeny.

Given our current knowledge we cannot, with authenticity and integrity, sustain the same relationship to the DoSOs that we have done for many centuries. If we want to see the sparkle in the eyes of our children, if we want them to be proud to be members of the BAC group, if we want to give them a sense of purpose and hope, if we want to be proud of ourselves as parents and of the legacies we have created then we need to develop, as BACs, a collective will to exist in our own right as a distinctive ethnic group. This is an imperative if we are to experience the fruit of our own self-consciousness as opposed to living by the dictates of that of another ethnic group. Ending our own psychological slavery takes away the option of blame and calls for taking on personal responsibility. Although psychological slavery became oppressive for me, for many of us DoEAs it actually provides a safe environment. It is a place in the world we know and feel safe even if it leaves us without self-respect. The DoEAs must make the choice: fat slavery or lean freedom.

The call to unity under the umbrella of BAC is a call to self and group exploration facilitating our clipped wings to grow again instead of creating a defensive ethnic enclave from which to view other ethnic groups suspiciously. A parochial defensive enclave is not the destiny of the DoEAs. Ours is a higher calling towards the goal of co-existence, cross-fertilisation, dialogue and exchange, rather than isolation, separation and delineation. Because we are intrinsic components of British culture and have been for 500 years we have the capacity for changing it through changing ourselves, as discussed in chapter seven.

Embracing slavery

> To be real you need to celebrate your own history, humble and tormented as it might be, and the history of your own parents and grandparents, howsoever that history might be marked by scars and mistakes. It is the only history you will ever have; reject it and you reject yourself. (Gatto, 2002)

I was helped in the process of moving beyond the shame of slavery which kept me in denial of this history, by Caroline Myss (2002) who, builds on Jung's work with archetypes (Boeree, 2006). Myss (2002) cites Jung as arguing that archetypes provide the foundation for our personality, our drives, feelings, beliefs, motivations and actions. Myss describes how archetypal patterns provide clear insights into an individual's psyche in that the archetypes are patterns of intelligence, dynamic living forms of energy that are shared in many people's thoughts and emotions across cultures and countries. Interestingly, Myss (2002) identifies the slave archetype as representing a complete absence of the power of choice and self-authority. However, she acknowledges that it is precisely the absence of willpower that gives the slave the potential for personal transformation. Myss identifies the ultimate spiritual task for those who are carriers of the slave archetype as surrendering their will to the Divine and to become a Divine Slave. She acknowledges the experience of the DoEAs for whom the slave archetype carries a level of historic freight that is impossible to overlook.

Myss argues that those of us for whom slavery is a part of our genetic history need to take a close look at the possible presence of the slave archetype in our intimate family. Those who dismiss this archetype as having no role in their lives may discover that it is more prevalent than they imagine, because of its many different expressions. Myss uses the example of a soldier armed with weapon as a slave because soldiers, like slaves, follow orders unconditionally especially when these orders violate personal integrity. We witnessed this in the black experience in organisational life in chapter three and in terms of black socialisation as an ongoing process in British society. Others may manipulate the slave like a puppet, regardless of how the archetype manifests. However, the core learning of the slave archetype is to understand the paradoxical truth that you are only truly free when you have surrendered all power of choice to the Divine, which in our case, as the DoEAs, is our own self-consciousness.

This is the answer to D'Anguiar's question in chapter one: how long shall the master's daylight continue to rule over our nights? The master's daylight will continue to rule over our nights for as along as the consciousness of the slave owner continues to rule over our consciousness as the DoEAs. The primary task we have today is to attain integrity in our inner life. I have shown that it has been the primacy of the internalised white consciousness over my own self-consciousness that had to be destabilised and dethroned. DuBois made this now famous statement in 1903:

> After the Egyptian and the Indian, the Greek and Roman, the Teuton and Mongolian, the Negro is a sort of seventh son, born with a veil and gifted with second sight in this American world – a world which yields him no true self-consciousness, but only lets him see himself through the revelation of the other world. It is a peculiar sensation, this double consciousness, this sense of always looking at one's self through the eyes of others, of measuring one's soul by the tape of a world that looks on in amused contempt and pity ... One ever feels his twoness – an American, a Negro: two souls, two thoughts, two unreconciled strivings; two warring ideals in one dark body, whose dogged strength alone keeps it from being torn asunder. The history of the American Negro is the history of this strife – this longing to attain self-conscious manhood to merge his double self into a better and truer self.

Lincoln (1995) contributes to this idea when he acknowledges that with the depersonalisation through slavery of enslaved Africans

> ... only spiritual identity remained, and on that slender filament the reconstruction of the African sense of self would ultimately depend ... As we must look to Africa to find the roots of the process which stripped (the DoEA) of their identity, so must we also look to Africa for the primary sources of its restoration. Critical to this task is some understanding of the West African religious cosmos ...

As we move forward with a renewed sense of self, van Dijk's (1993) observation takes on a poignancy that is of particular importance to our situation:

> ... only when social groups themselves, such as minority groups in the case of opinion formation about ethnic affairs, take the initiative and are able to expropriate some elements of dominant group power are they also able to propose a redefinition of the situation that may be adopted (and adapted) by some white elite groups and organisations, which in turn may become increasingly legitimate in the media, thereby contributing to a change of consensus.

DoEAs claiming our British identity

An important part of the above process is to acknowledge the British influence on our identity. This idea is seen as contentious by some DoEAs because of the pain and anger felt about the treatment of our ancestors and the ongoing stigmatisation of our identity by Caucasians. However, acknowledging the impact of British culture on our life is critical to the process of developing conscious bicultural competence. Denial of British cultural influence on the DoEAs can best be understood as the emotional response of those trapped in the unconscious bicultural competence quadrant of Figure 8.1. It was only by acknowledging British culture, as opposed to eclipsing it as something separate to me, that I was able to surface and recognise black culture as a primary subculture of British culture. Reasons for taking on the British identifier include:

- Moving our children and ourselves beyond the cultural limbo of having no physical place we acknowledge as 'home'

- Acknowledging responsibilities and obligations of citizenship, which is not possible when our relationship with Britain is unaccepted or unrealised

- Acknowledging ourselves as co-creators of British culture

- Keeping British culture and its dehumanising qualities at the forefront of our consciousness in terms of our responsibility in working with it

Issues for the TMP(bac)

It did not really matter what we expected from life, but rather what life expected from us ... Life ultimately means taking the responsibility to find the right answer to its problems and to fulfil the tasks which it constantly sets for each individual. (Frankl, 1984:98)

Issues that the TMP(bac) have to work with have been grouped under five key themes, which have repeatedly occurred throughout this analysis, forming the 'power' acronym (Figure 10.2 below). These are the basis of the work underpinning the *Metanoia* Project(bac)[2007-2034] spearheading transformational change in years to come. The Centre for British African-Caribbean Studies, operating as an education and research resource centre, supports this work.

Figure 10.2: Themes for re-humanising the DoEAs

Perspective transformation/culture as inner experience

Overcoming through bicultural socialisation/competence

Working with issues of identity

Education for human living

Research as a source of self-knowledge/future-visioning

Perspective transformation/culture as inner experience

Frankl (1984) offers the DoEAs an important and different perspective on life when he argues that the question we could be asking is: what does Life expect of us instead of the more commonly asked question what do I expect of Life? Life seems to be saying to us as a group that we must attend to the inner culture of the members of our group, this being the crucial outcome of culture. The inner culture achieved by our group members is the most promising indicator of the quality of our external culture as seen in our everyday lives. In ensuring that our members acquire needed sources of strength Frankl points us towards seeing life as an opportunity and a challenge. The perspective transformation required is to enable the DoEAs to make a victory of experience. BAC members facilitated towards turning life into an inner triumph instead of ignoring the challenge and simply vegetating, as so many do, achieve a perspective transformation.

DoEAs will also be facilitated away from living out what Frankl calls a 'provisional existence' where current life experiences are seen as something to endure until such time as real life begins. This is instead of understanding life experiences as opportunities to grow spiritually beyond current conceptions of self. The DoEAs will be taken back in time to Africa, the enslavement of our ancestors and slavery on the Caribbean plantations to our current position in British society, so helping its members to give their lives meaning and purpose, instead of repressing and avoiding our history. We can begin redeeming our history so that we no longer live lives of shame and avoidance, and recognise the consequences of this for our inner lives. Understanding that we live in what Goldsmith (1963) refers to as a parenthesis in eternity is critical to this perspective transformation. Our lives are a moment in time and so it is important that we really live and create life-enhancing legacies for those who come after us.

Overcoming with bicultural socialisation/competence

There has been clear evidence that the primary problem for the DoEAs as a group is that we do not engage in the bicultural socialisation that other ethnic minority groups have understood is crucial to the life success of minority groups living away from home. We do not engage in the process of ethnic identity development. This would provide our members with an alternative life-enhancing design for living that enables them to respond effectively to the challenges which are presented by being socialised into British culture and society with its two oppositional subcultures. Unlike the Jews, the DoEAs have not learned to make sacred the transmission of culture by teaching our children who they are, their place in the world and how to relate to other social groups. We have left this vital process of shaping the inner culture of our membership to the DoSOs who are unaware of how the shaping process worked in slavery and how it continues to work in a post-colonial society. We are also largely unaware of our own involvement in the negative outcomes which are detailed throughout. The process of engaging in bicultural socialisation and ethnic identity development will support the DoEAs in embracing our history and understanding our relationship to British culture. DoEAs will only see the need to educate our young when we have a body of knowledge that we want to be transmitted down our generational chain. TMP(bac) prepares DoEAs for working with these issues as a means of working through possible conflict with the ethnic majority.

Working with issues of identity

The outcome of this bicultural socialisation failure on our part is that British culture continues to unconsciously co-opt the DoEAs into the cultural world of the DoSOs and their ways of viewing enslaved Africans which the DoEAs have learned to accommodate. The critical issue in terms of identity is working with the foreclosure of our identity as blacks and the outcome of this for us as a group. Unconsciousness has prevented us from understanding the ways in which slavery and the colonial and imperial regimes foreclosed, through the imposition of different races (Erikson, 1950) and a negative black identity, the widespread acquisition of strengths of character in the DoEAs enabling us to take charge of our own lives. The significant word here is 'widespread' as it relates to 'community' and the sources of strength that community can provide individuals. Instead divisions were put in place resulting in disunity between enslaved Africans which still continues through to today. This ensures the loyalties of the DoEAs are given to the DoSOs while distrust continues to be bred between the psychologically enslaved because of our unconsciousness. Psuedo speciation has also ensured the premature foreclosure of the identity of the DoEAs, who have, in the main, become locked into the black identity externally imposed on us. Catalysts need to be put in place to interrupt this identity foreclosure so that the identity formation process can be engaged with by the DoEAs, enabling its members to come to the point of the achieved identity that is our right.

Education for human living/ending fear

The key insight of chapter five is that as human beings we have important intrinsic qualities that make us unique and wonderful in our own right and that by living according to these qualities, instead of inside the black culture of victimhood and deprivation, we have the power to transform our life experience. Most of the theorisation of the black experience views our lives from within the fixed boundaries of race and, therefore, the black-white duality. Consequently, solutions can only also be identified within these fixed and pathological boundaries. In this process I made the invisible visible as I revealed the inner black culture the institution of social interaction and the characteristic features of slavery so that they could be consciously and deliberately worked with. Gatto (2002) reminds us that real education is not about money but is an internally generated effort consisting of insight, power, understanding and self-control, all of which exist outside the cash economy.

Research as a source of self-knowledge

Researching is the act of engaging with life to search and search again until we find something that approximates the inner truth we are seeking. Realising that we have not yet really lived as the DoEAs we no longer seek to move from the black box to the white box, as shown in Figure 10.1. Instead, we seek to find ourselves and our own destiny as BACs in the assurance that our clipped wings can indeed fly again. The collective purpose and meaning that accrues from researching into our life experiences will surface patterns and tracks that have hitherto gone unnoticed (facilitated through CBACS). Implementing lifecycle theory will be instrumental in supporting us in reflecting together on what it means to be BAC and will result in the development of a collective purpose and meaning for the group. Our members will codify the culture being developed for transmission across the generations to facilitate the evolvement of the members of our group. Researching our life experiences reveals inner knowledge and the contribution we have to make to the world as a group. We need not only to protect our gene pool but also our ideas pool just like other ethnic groups do (St. Aubin, 2004). Through research the DoEAs can be helped towards moving away from a position of self-pity towards engaging with the recovery work, the human task, of creating functional lives for our progeny and ourselves as we begin to recognise the responsibilities we have to our group as a whole.

Learning from feedback from other ethnic groups

In addition to taking lessons from the knowledge of the ages, Kotkins (1993) identified one of the success strategies of tribes set to dominate the 21st century as that of developing a willingness to learn from other cultures. In this final section observations of individuals from other ethnic groups which give BACs insights into our own lives are included for further reflection. Doing this enables us to move beyond the parochialities and atomisation that black culture has been criticised for.

African-American, Dr Walter Massey, President of Morehouse College (Mamon, 2003):

We should

- establish a firm research base
- support black teachers
- identify success areas
- address the issue of economic development as a whole
- engage our young men

British, Stephen Twigg (Mamon, 2003):

- Black parents, although historically marginalised, are key to improving the achievement of their own children in the school system

Chinese (Foreign Despatches, 2005):

- stay as psychologically separate as possible from whites
- overturn our dysfunctional adaptation to the culture of poverty within which we live
- note our lack of common sense in investing in an education system that is clearly failing us as a group

McWhorter (2001):

- Blacks caught up in a culture of victimhood; self-sabotaging behaviours; anti-intellectualism and separatism.

Dane (Holdt, 1997):

- black underachievement results from the inability of whites to visualise blacks as emancipated free human beings
- leads to white disillusionment resulting in a racist scapegoat fixation on blacks and not in their own stunting relationship to that group
- slavery and colonialism's evil circle is carried on indefinitely through the giving of paternalism without attempting therapeutic treatment of the racism in the donor

American (Widdowson, 2001):

- blacks have been unable to form a cohesive entity and so draw strength from pride in some distinctive set of beliefs
- no history of self-help like other ethnic minorities
- blacks are trapped in a self-reinforcing cycle in which economic failure has seemed to justify and perpetuate the attitudes that contribute to that economic failure
- This cannot just be attributed to white racism but also to black continuing atomisation and lack of confidence

Asian (Madood, 2002):

- Becoming overly integrated with the British has not worked to black advantage
- Warns other ethnic groups to avoid this until they have achieved at least middle class status

These statements affirm an experience we are aware of but which is typically denied within the boundaries of the black-white duality of everyday life. They support the findings of my research as well as the solutions I have experientially developed. These confirmations from onlookers of the black-white duality support my thesis that this black-white duality must be ended and that the catalyst for achieving this must be for the DoEAs to take the necessary steps to renege on the black identity. To achieve this we must act now, contradicting Alleyne's (2004) finding in chapter two that blacks tend to be non-actional.

Generative educators

The chapter looks to a transcendent vision for BACs as an ethnic group enabling our clipped wings to fly again. TMP(bac) spearheads this vision through its commitment to attending to the spiritual hygiene of the DoEAs as an ethnic group. The BAC identifier has been surfaced as the appropriate ethnic and cultural identity for the DoEAs and the symbolic home offering them nurture, solace, healing and community. In this space BAC members can start to foster our inner life as a means of achieving our individual and group potential. In so doing so we are also protecting ourselves, and especially our children, from powerful external forces at work to prevent us achieving the quality of life to which we aspire. When DoEAs and DoSOs work together, using the five-dimensional human being model (figure 5.2, p69) and the bi-cultural competence matrix (figure 8.1, p118) as tools of authentic human development, they are furthering humanity and dissolving the wall of silence and dysfunction that surrounds us.

11

The monster speaks ... of knowledge, history, culture, identity and power

...a people with a past infused by oppression and suffering is charged with a special responsibility, to remember and remind: to redeem that past with a creative meaning; to recognise and insist that we must treat one another as equally human, beyond differences of race or nationality, religion or culture, if we are not to become mere beasts that talk. (Segal, 1995: pxii)

The worst realities of our age are manufactured realities. It is therefore our task, as creative participants in the universe, to redream our world. The fact of possessing imaginations means that everything can be redreamed. Each reality can have its alternative possibilities. Human beings are blessed with the necessity of transformation. (Okri, 1997)

The future is not a result of choices among alternative paths offered by the present, but a place that is created – created first in the mind and will, created next in activity. The future is not some place we are going to, but one we are creating. The paths are not to be found, but made, and the activity of making them, changes both the maker and the destination. (James, 2005)

Introduction

In this final chapter I reflect on the contributions this book makes to the educational practice of teachers in general and parents of British African-Caribbean children in particular. Firstly, I do not assume that the DoSOs are maliciously engaged in keeping the DoEAs in a subordinated position. Rather, the mechanisms put in place during slavery have taken on a life of their own. Back in the 19th century there were no armies of counsellors available to treat both the DoEAs and the DoSOs for the trauma we had differentially undergone. The issues were therefore pushed underground where they have been simmering ever since. Had I not done the work to surface how the black white duality is perpetuated, it might well have persisted. I have argued that those of us charged with the responsibility of educating future generations are cultural practitioners, educationalists and academics. It is we who have the responsibility of being conscious of the culture we are transmitting and why. Culture is ongoing process and that we can no longer blindly protect and perpetuate a culture which has been built on dehumanisation since the building of the empire.

The solution is in the process

My purpose in sharing the process of my research journey has been to provide insights into how attention to the process itself reveals the solutions to the issues we are struggling with. Making the decision to stay with race as an issue proved to be countercultural and required me to make the further decision of whether to sacrifice my life to the culture of silence. Instead I chose to expose the culture of silence that is detrimental to our well-being. I developed autobiographical awareness-in-action which enabled me to take informed action in the world. Attention to process facilitates taking one step at a time through our suffering as opposed to denial and avoidance.

The bigger lesson that has come through attending to process is that 'the culture' we blame for our problems is one we participate in making. Unconsciousness of this fact was necessary for my participation in my own oppression. Unconsciousness meant that I could only perpetuate the *status quo*. Attention to process gave me strength. It broke me out of unconsciousness into consciousness and into awareness of the role I was playing. I have continued to use attention to process to take informed action through striving towards being the change I want to see. It is my hope that other educators will grasp the spirit that underlies the content of this book to realise how attention to the process of their own lives can facilitate them towards being the change they want to see. Realising my position on the unconscious bicultural competence quadrant in Figure 8.1, I was presented with the challenge of what to do about it. Sharing the process I have undergone enables readers to reflect on their own likely position and think: what will I do now?

Re-humanising British culture

Figure 11.1 below summarises the lessons I have learned about race in Britain, as seen in each chapter. Figure 11.2 (p191) summarises the vision for British culture in terms of how it will be.

Figure 11.1: Features of a de-humanised British culture

British Ethnic Culture

(presented as the 'integrated' community)

↓

White Culture – superior culture

(White silence)

(British-English culture repressed)

Defensiveness on the part of whites; denial; fear; distancing; power moves

Structuring within culture via politics of positionality

Social distance boundary line drawings

Characteristic features of the institution of chattel slavery

↓

SILENCE/DENIAL/UNAWARENESS/ IGNORANCE/GUILT/FEAR/SHAME DISTRUST/AVOIDANCE/REPRESSION

↓

Black Culture – DoEAs – victim/soul murder culture

(Black complicity)

Socialisation administered by whites (racism, discrimination, etc)

(unconscious assimilation/normalisation – silence)

Lack of self-knowledge; 'educated' by ethnic majority for unconsciousness

Decentred in terms of ethnic culture and lacking centricity in education

Accommodation on the part of blacks; appeasement; survival; fear;

(British African-Caribbean culture -authentic culture – concealed)

(Non-white ethnic minorities protected by ethnic cultures)

Recognising the wall of silence, ignorance, distrust, fear, blame and a host of other negative emotions that underpins the 'deafening silence' identified by Matsuura (2004) as surrounding slavery and the black experience is critical to understanding Figure 11.1. These are the issues I have engaged with on my own research journey over the last eighteen years in the process of learning what it means to be black so that I could make a contribution to this experience as an educator. The answers that surfaced as I engaged experientially with the issues, seeking to transform them in my own life-world are seen in Figure 11.2.

Figure 11.2: Features of a re-humanised British culture

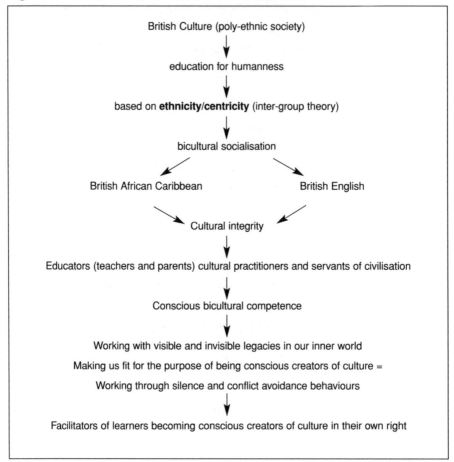

The issue of the 'black community' is not a black problem after all but a societal problem. But I know now that I cannot sit back any longer and wait for the DoSOs to correct the injustices of the situation. I am a *bona fide* member of British society and have the responsibility to be an active citizen, especially in my role as a cultural practitioner in the British education system.

Sharing the process of my journey I have revealed that the answers to our problems are right there in those aspects of our lives we deny and avoid instead of facing. The solution to the problems of race and human life unfolded as I moved beyond silence and conflict avoidance to engage with the fundamental task of human life: being conscious creators of culture. I started to see that which we are socialised not to see much less to articulate. These were the very things that were inhibiting my life in Britain. At first it all felt too much for me. Working with myself however towards the goal of authenticity and personal integrity opened up possibilities as I realised that changing myself was vital to bringing about wider change. Figure 11.2 outlines the various changes I made. First, I named British society for what it is: a poly-ethnic society (Barth, 1969). I challenged myself to name myself as a DoEA so I could embrace the legacy instead of being ashamed of it. And I named the ethnic majority as DoSOs. This helped me to begin to work with the issues I faced in my everyday life. Embracing the possibilities of what it means to be a whole human being as opposed to remaining subordinated to the ethnic majority stretched my comfort zone to create another preferred reality. And so the process of authentic human development evolved to the point it now has for me.

Putting the chapters of this book together has been an important and illuminating part of my research journey as I have surfaced, pieced together and consolidated understanding of the different parts of a complex jigsaw that has evolved over hundreds of years. The five themes identified in the title of this chapter are crucial to understanding the black experience in Britain. Despite all my education I was lacking in all five. Through engaging in real education for my PhD with real as an acronym for relevant, educational, action-oriented and liberating I have wakened out of the sleep of unconsciousness depicted on the bicultural competence matrix (Figure 8.1) to witness my true condition. Today I am no longer the unconscious monster created by slave owners, psychologically bound to their descendants through the black-white duality. I have become my own person. What has evolved from my research is a distinctive BAC perspective – the perspective of those DoEAs who have broken out of the foreclosed black identity of an externally imposed cultural disorder to arrive at an achieved identity.

My despair when I started my research journey has been replaced by my engagement with the five themes identified in this chapter. I have gained insight, understanding and discernment. I have developed practice wisdom from embracing Gandhi's famous idea: be the change you want to see. The change can be seen in the reconfiguration of British society (see Figure 6.2) beyond black and white as seen in Figure 11.3 overleaf.

Educators developing our own authentic projects of being
Becoming aware of myself as an educator as part of a larger purpose and engaged in the project of furthering humanity, I am now in the process of developing my own authentic project of being. Each of us has an important role to play in furthering humanity where race and social inequality is concerned. Each of our lives is part of the long revolution towards realising the destiny of culture. To this end we must create a human culture supportive of

Figure 11.3 A reconfigured poly-ethnic British society that as moved beyond black and white

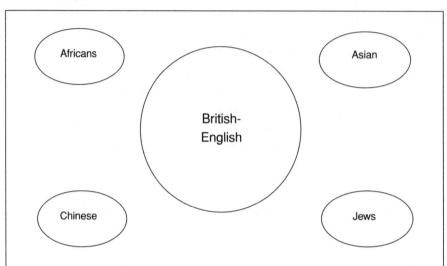

all members of the human race and not just our own group, as currently seen in the dysfunctional workings of British culture with its two subcultures. The survival of our planet depends on balance and yet the human family has been off balance since the institution of slavery in the 16th century and the growth of the British Empire. It is incumbent on us as the DoEAs and DoSOs to wake up out of the sleep of unconsciousness so that cosmic balance can be restored. As the DoEAs and DoSOs we have important healing work to do. This begins with ourselves. The world is now in need of the ideas that have been fermenting in us as part of the historical process.

As we break out of conditioned, conforming behaviours we move towards developing our own authentic project of being. In my own case, embracing the BAC perspective has ended my unconscious involvement in the oppositional relationship of the black-white duality. It has also given me a transcendent vantage point from which to witness the black-white duality at work. It reminds me not to continue to allow racialised emotions, a product of the black-white duality, to drain my emotional energies. Instead I focus my energies on my goal of being a proactive cultural worker in the field of higher education where I position myself as an elder of the BAC community acting as an intergenerational buffer and working to prevent the ongoing transmission of a dysfunctional cultural legacy to both the DoEAs and DoSOs (Kotre, 1983).

Looking to the future

The re-education and the re-humanising agenda are not concocted ideas but the choiceless choice that is necessary at this point of our history. Consequently, the CBACS and TMP(teach) and TMP(bac) are natural outcomes of the lessons learned from the process. It is apparent that this agenda should also be spearheaded by British African-Caribbeans.

a) Centre for British African-Caribbean Studies (www.cbacs.org)

The work of the Centre includes:

- Continuing to develop a BAC perspective using the lessons of slavery, the context of BAC recreation, in terms of knowledge, history, culture, identity and power and applying them to the future so that we build a world where tolerance, equality and diversity are celebrated (Mac Taggart, 2004)

- Working with the human costs of living in a culture of silence, fear and shame by facilitating individuals and groups through the quadrants of the bicultural competence matrix (Figure 8.1) towards the goal of conscious bicultural competence and in the process engage with these outcomes (see The *Metanoia* Project[2007-2034] below)

- Surfacing new knowledge and so developing a research base on the nature of black and white cultures and the resultant black-white duality as we move towards British-English and British African-Caribbean cultures as alternatives

- Equipping DoEAs with the tools to claim the rights of freedom (Beals and Spindler, 1973) which include empirical research on ethnic identity development amongst the DoEAs. This includes understanding the power of talk-as-interaction

- Working with the lived experiences of DoEAs in remembering, understanding and applying the lessons of the legacies of slavery to the future

The Centre for British African Caribbean Studies (CBACS) focuses on what can be learned from the 500 years that has elapsed since the creation of the institution of slavery in the Caribbean under British rule. This enables the DoEAs and the DoSOs to study their shared history. It also provides the margin of space for the DoEAs that Elkins (1968) identifies as being crucial to resisting slavery. It also facilitates the development of a broader and richer BAC culture and identity than is possible within the limitations of black culture. The DoEAs have evolved in different ways since the enslavement of our ancestors. Bringing these experiences together under the banner of the BAC identity will open up possibilities for the DoEAs as a group. Previous chapters have raised important issues that the CBACS has already started to work with.

b) The *Metanoia Project*[2007-2034]

At the heart of The Metanoia Project is the particular *metanoia* I achieved in being able to see the DoEAs and the DoSOs as members of one race and to realise that the oppositional but symbiotic relationship that exists between members of the two groups is the result of the black-white duality. The *Metanoia* Project focuses therefore on bringing together the knowledge developed over the course of this research (1989 to present) to work with both DoSOs and DoEAs to understand the nature of the black-white duality, how we have all become complicit in maintaining it and what we can do to dismantle it. The *Metanoia* Project is an ethical project concerned with healing relationships. In the context of this book focus has been placed on teachers at all levels of the education system and how they relate interpersonally: DoSOs to DoEAs as well as the DoEA to DoEA. This healing work is important if teachers and the BAC community are the critical agents for bringing about wider change in British society.

New beginnings

Sharing this work has been the action research commitment I made many years ago to make my work public. In the process I have freed myself from the invisible legacies of slavery which I could not work with because I was blind to or in fear of them and so have been unconsciously responsible for transmitting generationally. Now that I have awareness I recognise my responsibility to create a culture within which I am at the centre stage of my own life living choicefully.

I have learned that knowing how to be human, how to live humanly with other members of the human race is not a destination but an everyday challenge. Daily, I find myself surrounded by family, friends, students and colleagues who know little about what it means to be fully human because they have been conditioned to live automatically in a monolithic and fixed world. I see that the BAC perspective which has evolved out of this research has given me important insights on how to live that others need today. All around people are in various forms of slavery but are unaware of it. We all have life challenges: the question is how will we deal with them? The DoEAs and DoSOs have been trapped in a dark age kept in place by the black-white duality, a product of the institutionalisation of slavery. Widdowson (2001) speaks of dark ages thus:

Dark ages imply renewal and growth. After a dark age, the old civilisation is never simply revived. There is a qualitatively new configuration, and this is largely discontinuous with what went before. The longer and deeper the dark age, the more radical the new configuration. That is to say, significant change requires a significant dark age. The place where destruction begins and proceeds the furthest is likely to make the earliest and most complete recovery. This is the phoenix principle. Catastrophe comes before progress. One cannot occur without the other and the greater the catastrophe, the greater the progress ... People need to sleep and to dream. It is how their minds reconcile each day's experiences into some sort of order ... Just as forest fires refresh the forest, clearing out debris and allowing new life to break through, so dark ages renew the historical process, clearing away outmoded institutions and giving the opportunity for other cultures and fresh ideas to make headway.

The British African-Caribbean perspective, born out of engaging with the legacies of slavery, is a sign of new life breaking through.

Glossary

Blacks and Whites – the names, respectively, given to enslaved Africans and slave-owners on the plantations of the Caribbean as a means of establishing power differentials between members of the two groups. Blacks exist in a politics of positionality relative to whites

Black-white duality – the dysfunctional symbiotic oppositional relationship which has developed over time between blacks and whites

Black and white cultures – the designs for living that evolved from the imposition of external cultural disorders on enslaved Africans and enslaving Europeans.

British African-Caribbeans (BAC) – the ethnic identifier of the DoEAs but which is repressed behind the more common identifier of 'blacks'

Centre for British African-Caribbean Studies (CBACS) – a research and education resource centre that applies knowledge to the BAC experience with the aim of transformation and self-renewal

Culture – the differential design for living that emerges from the self-consciousness of a people based on human interaction and choice

Descendants of enslaved Africans (DoEAs) – the progeny of those Africans who were enslaved and brought to British colonies in the Caribbean

Descendants of slave owners (DoSOs) – the progeny of former slave owners as well as those Caucasians who have, wittingly and unwittingly, given up their ethnic identity in order to participate in the privileges that accrue to whites

Race – the social construction based on skin colour developed to put in place power differentials between enslaved Africans and enslaving Europeans.

Bibliography

Acker, S (1994) *Gendered Education: Sociological Perspectives on Women, Teaching and Feminism,* OUP

Adams, K (2002) At the Table with Arendt: Toward a Self-Interested Practice of Coalition Discourse in *Hypatia,* Volume 17, Number 1

Alchin, N (2003) *Theory of Knowledge,* John Murray Publishers, London

Alcoff, L M (1998) What should white people do? *Hypatia,* Volume 13, Number 3, http://www. iupress.indiana.edu/journals/hypatia/hyp13-3.html

Alderfer, C P (1998) A Group Psychological Perspective on Multiculturalism: What Will It Take for the High Priests and Priestesses to Change Their Minds? in *Workplace Diversity: Issues and Perspectives,* (ed) Alfrieda Daly

Alderfer, Clayton P. and Kenwyn K. Smith (1982) 'Studying intergroup relations embedded in organizations,' *Administrative Science Quarterly,* 27, 35-65

Alfred, M V (1997) A Reconceptualisation of Marginality: Perspectives of African-American Female Faculty in the White Academy, 27th Annual SCRUTEA Conference Proceedings, Education-line, http://www.leeds.ac.uk/educol/documents

Alleyne, A (2004) *Black Identity and Workplace Oppression,* www.allaboutpsychotherapy.com

Anderson, G T (1977) The Past is Always Present: How your life is influenced by ideas and events of the past, Review and Herald Publishing Association, USA

Ani, M (1994) *Yurugu: An African-Centered Critique of European Cultural Thought and Behaviour,* Africa World Press

Argyris, C and Schon, D A (1996) *Organisational Learning II: Theory, Method and Practice,* Addison-Wesley Publishing Company

Armah, A K (1978) *The Healers: an historical novel,* Heinemann

Asante, M K (1992) *Afrocentricity,* Africa World Press, Inc. 5th Edition

Asante, M K (1991) The Afrocentric Idea in Education in *Modern Black Nationalism: From Marcus Garvey to Louis Farrakhan* (ed) W L Van Deburg, New York University Press, New York and London

Bales, K (1999) *Disposable People: New Slavery in the Global Economy,* University of California Press, USA

Banton, M (1997) *Ethnic and Racial Consciousness,* Longman, London and New York

Barth, F (1969) (Ed) *Ethnic groups and boundaries,* Bergen, Norway: Universitets Forlaget

Bateson, G (1972) *Steps to an Ecology of Mind: A Revolutionary Approach to Man's Understanding of Himself,* Ballantine Books: New York

Beals, A R and Spindler, G L (1973) *Culture in Process* (2nd Edition) Hot, Rinehart and Winston Inc

Bennet, L Jr (1985) *Before the Mayflower: A History of Black America*, Penguin Books

Berardinelli, J (1994) Mary Shelly's Frankenstein, A Film Review, http://movie-reviews.colossus. net/movies/m/mary_shellys.html

Bergenhenegouwen, G (1987) Hidden Curriculum in the University, *Higher Education* 16(2) 535-543

Biko, F (1996) Introduction to African World Studies: Nile Valley Civilisations: Problems and Positions – Handouts Term 1, The Khepera Institute

Blauner, R (1972) *Racial Oppression in America*, Harper and Row

Boeree, C G (2006) Personality Theories: Carl Jung 1875-1961, http://webspace.ship.edu/cgboer/ jung.html

Bowles, M L (1990) Recognising Deep Structures in Organisations, *Organisation Studies*, 11(3) pp395-412

Bravette, G (1997) Towards Bicultural Competence: Researching for Personal and Professional Transformations, Unpublished PhD Thesis, University of Bath, UK

Bravette, G (1996) Reflections on a Black Woman's Management Learning, *Women in Management Review*, MCB University Press, Vol 11(3)

Bravette, G (1994) Black Women Managers and Participatory Action Research, World Congress 3 on Action Learning, Action Research and Process Management, University of Bath, England

Bravette, G (1993) Unleashing Human Potential: Emancipatory Action Research and Black Women Managers, unpublished MBA dissertation, South Bank University, London

Brodkin, K (1998) *How the Jews became White folks and what that says about race in America*, New Brunswick, NJ: Rutgers University Press

Buccholz R and Rosenthal, S B (1998) *Business Ethics: The Pragmatic Path Beyond Principles to Process*, Prentice Hall, NJ

Burke, A W (1986) *Racism, Prejudice and Mental Illness in Transcultural Psychiatry* (ed) John L Cox, Croon Helm, London

Byrne, E (1978) *Women and Education*, Tavistock: London

Campbell, H (1999) No Mass Tribute for a Hero, http://www.hartford-hwp.com/archives/43/129.html

Carter, J H (1994) Racism's Impact on Mental Health, *Journal of the National Medical Association*, 86(7), pp543-547

Carter, B; Harris, C and Joshi, S (1987) The 1951-55 Conservative Government and the Racialisation of Black Immigration, *Policy Papers in Ethnic Relations, No 11*, Centre for Research on Ethnic Relations

Cashmore, E (1988) *Dictionary of Race and Ethnic Relations*, Routledge (2nd edition)

Cashmore, E (1989) *United Kingdom: Class, Race and Gender since the War*, Unwin Hyman, London

Cashmore, E (1997) *The Black Culture Industry*, Routledge: London and New York

Chile, L M and Simpson, G (2004) Spirituality and Community Development: Exploring the Link Between the Community and the Individual, *Community Development Journal*, Volume 39(4), Oxford University Press

Chisom, R and Washington, M (1997) *Undoing Racism: A Philosophy of International Social Change.* People's Institute Press: The People's Institute, 1444 North Johnson St., New Orleans, LA. 70116. Second Edition, pp. 30-31

Clarke, J H (1986) *Africa in the Ancient World, Kemet and the African Worldview: Research, Rescue and Restoration,* (eds) M Karenga and J Carruthers

Connerley, M L and Pedersen, P B (2005) *Leadership in a Diverse and Multicultural Environment: Developing Awareness, Knowledge and Skills,* Sage Publications Limited

Cooperrider, D and Whitney, D (1999) *A Positive Revolution in change: Appreciative Inquiry,* Taos, NM: Corporation for Positive Change

Cummins, J (1986) Empowering Minority Students: A Framework for Interventions, *Harvard Educational Review,* 56(1)

D'Aguiar, F (1994) *The Longest Memory,* Pantheon Books: New York

Dasberg, H (1991) Why we were silent – An Israeli Psychiatrist Speaks to Germans on Psychic Pain and Past Persecution, *Israeli Journal of Psychiatry and Related Science,* (28)2 p29-38

Davidson, B (1994) *The Search for Africa: A History in the Making,* James Curry

Davidson, M N (2001) Know thine adversary: the impact of race on styles of dealing with conflict, *Sex Roles,* Volume 45(5/6), p259-276, Plenum Publishing Corporation

DeAnda, D (1984) Bicultural Socialisation: Factors Affecting the Minority Experience, *Social Work,* 29(3) March/April, pp101-105

Department for Education and Skills (DES) (2003) *Aiming High: Raising the Achievement of Minority Ethnic Pupils,* Ref DfES/0183/2003

Dewey, J (1934) *Individual psychology and education, The Philosopher,* Volume XII, http://www.the-philosopher.co.uk/dewey.htm

Dhruev, N (1992) Conflict and Race in Social Work Relations, *Journal of Social Work Practice,* Vol 6:1

Dickens, F and Dickens, J B (1991) *The Black Manager: Making it in the Corporate World,* Amacom (American Management Association)

Diop, C A (1974) *The African Origin of Civilisation: Myth or Reality,* Lawrence Hill Books

DuBois, W E B (1903) *The Souls of Black Folk,* A Signet Classic Reprint (1995)

Eisler, R (1991) *Social Transformation and the Feminine: From Domination to Partnership, To Be a Woman: The Birth of the Conscious Feminine,* (ed) C Zweig, Mandala

Elder, L and Paul, R (2004) *The Miniature Guide to Taking Care of the Human Mind: How it Learns and How it Mislearns,* The Foundation for Critical Thinking

Elkin, S (1968) *Slavery, A Problem in American Institutional and Intellectual Life,* University of Chicago Press, 2nd edition

Emerson, R W (1995) *Self-Reliance and Other Essays,* Barnes and Noble Books

Erikson, Erik H. (1950) *Childhood and Society.* New York: W. W. Norton

Fals Border, O (1979) Investigating reality in order to transform it: the Columbian experience, *Dialectical Anthropology,* 4, 35-55

Fantasia, R and Hirsch, E L (1995) Culture in Rebellion: The Appropriation and Transformation of the Veil in the Algerian Revolution, *Social Movements and Culture,* (eds) H Johnston and B Klandermans, Regents of the University of Minnesota

Feagin, J (2000) *Racist America*, New York: Routledge

Ferguson, N (2004) *Empire: How Britain Made the Modern World*, Penguin Books

Fernandes, L (1990) *Academic Freedom*, Zed Books in association with the World University Service

Fernando, S (1996) Black people working in white institutions: lessons from personal experience, *Human Systems: The Journal of Systemic Consultation and Management*, 7(2-3), 143-154

Foner, N (1977) The Jamaicans: Cultural and Social Change Among Migrants in Britain (chapter 5), *Between Two Cultures: Migrants and Minorities in Britain*, J L Watson (ed), Basil Blackwell

Fordham, S (1996) *Blacked Out: Dilemmas of Race, Identity and Success at Capital High*, The University of Chicago Press

Fordham, S (1991) Peer-Proofing Academic Competition Among Black Adolescents 'Acting White' Black American Style, in *Empowerment Through Multicultural Education* (ed) C E Sleeter, State University of New York Press

Foreign Dispatches (2005) Random Remarks on Current Affairs: Black underachievement in context, http://foreigndispatches.typepad.com/dispatches/2005/03/black_underachi.html

Fox, K (2005) *Watching the English: The Hidden Rules of English Behaviour: The Hidden Rules of English Behaviour*, Hodder and Stoughton Paperbacks

Francis, D and Woodcock, M (1996) *The New Unblocked Manager: A Practical Guide to Self-Development*, Gower

Frankenberg, R. (1993) *The Social Construction of Whiteness: White Women Race Matters*, University of Minnesota Press

Frankl, V (1984) *Man's Search for Meaning*, Washington Square Press, USA

Freire, P (1970) *Pedagogy of the Oppressed* (revised edition), Penguin Books

Fullan, M G (1993) Why teachers must become change agents, *Educational Leadership*, Volume 50(6)

Gatto, J T (2002) *A Different Kind of Teacher: Solving the Crisis of American Schooling*, Berkeley Hills Books, CA

Gergen, K J (1994) *Self Narration in Social Life, Realities and Relationships: Soundings in Social Construction*, Cambridge, Mass, Harvard University Press, chapter 8

Giles, R (1977) *The West Indian Experience in British Schools: Multi-Racial Education and Social Disadvantage in London*, Heineman Educational Books, London

Goldberg, D and Hodes, M (1992) The poison of racism and the self-poisoning of adolescents, *Journal of Family Therapy*, 14 pp61-67

Goldsmith, J S (1963) *A Parenthesis in Eternity: Living the Mystical Life*, Harper San Francisco

Gordon, G (2006) Transforming Thinking Amongst British African Caribbeans as an Academically Based Community Service Contribution, *Journal of Transformative Education*, Vol 4(3), pp 226-242, Sage Publications

Gordon, G (2005) Black Socialisation Defined and Characterised, Discussion Paper 3, *The 'Free Within Ourselves' Academically Based Community Service Research Project Paper Series*, London South Bank University

Gorringe, T J (2004) *Furthering Humanity: A Theology of Culture*, Ashgate

Gorski, P (1995) *Language of a Closet Racist: An Illustration*, http://www.edchange.org/multicultural/papers/langofracism2.html

Gossett, T F (1963) *Race: The history of an idea in America,* New York: Schocken

Gurnah, A (1987) Gatekeepers and caretakers: Swann, Scarman and the Social Policy of Containment, *Racial Inequality in Education,* (ed) B Troyna, Routledge

Hall, E T (1976) *Beyond Culture,* Anchor Press, Garden City, NJ

Haritatos, J and Benet-Martinez, V (2005) Bicultural Identity Integration (BII): Components and Psychosocial Antecedents, *Journal of Personality,* 73(4), 1015-1050

Harkavy, I (1997) *Universities and Community Schools,* (5)1-2 Fall-Winter 1997, University of Pennsylvania

Helms, J E (1990) *Black and White Racial Identity: Theory, Research and Practice,* Westport, CT: Greenwood Press

Heritage, J (2001) Goffman, Garfinkel and Conversation Analysis in *Discourse Theory and Practice: A Reader,* M Wetherell, S Taylor and S J Yates, Sage Publications, London

Hill Collins, P (2001) Like One of the Family: Race, Ethnicity and the Paradox of US National Identity, *Ethnic and Racial Studies,* (24)1, January 2001, p3-28

Hiro, D (1971) *Black British White British,* Eyre and Spottiswoode (Publishers) Ltd, Bristol

Hitchcock, J (2001) *Unravelling the White Cocoon,* Kendall/Hunt Publishers

Hoftstede, G (1980) *Cultures Consequences,* Sage, Beverly Hills, CA

Holdt, J (2002) American Pictures, http://www.american-pictures.com/

Holdt, J (1997) From an Unlearning Racism Workshop in Kenyon College, http://www.american-pictures.com/english/racism/workshop.html, accessed 10 August 2005

Home Office (2004) *Strength in Diversity: Towards A Community Cohesion and Race Equality Strategy,* http://www.homeoffice.gov.uk/documents/cons-strength-in-diverse-170904/strength-in-diversity-adults?view=Binary

hooks, b and West, C (1991) *Breaking Bread: Insurgent Black Intellectual Life,* South End Press, Boston, MA

Hoover, K; Marcia, J and Parris, K (1997) *The Power of Identity: Politics in a New Key,* Chatham House

Howard, G R (1999) *We Can't Teach What We Don't Know: White Teachers,* Multiracial Schools, Teachers College Press, US and UK

Howell, W S (1982) *The Empathic Communicator,* Belmont, CA:Wadsworth

Ignatiev, N (1995) *How the Irish became White,* New York: Routledge

James, C L R (1984) Africans and Afro-Caribbeans: A Personal View, *Ten,* Volume 8(16)

James, D (2005) http://www.life-with-confidence.com/confidencequotes.html

James, G G M (1992) *Stolen Legacy: Greek Philosophy is Stolen Egyptian Philosophy,* Africa World Press, Inc

Jay, G (2005) *Introduction to Whiteness Studies,* http://www.uwm.edu~gjay/Whiteness

Jenson, R (2005) *The Heart of Whiteness: Confronting Race, Racism and White Privilege,* City Lights

Jung, C. G. (1938) *Psychology and Religion* The Terry Lectures. New Haven: Yale University Press. (contained in Psychology and Religion: West and East Collected Works Vol. 11

Kennedy, J (2004) Ethnic Minority Employment Task Force, Equality.Opportunity.Success. Year 1 Progress Report, Autumn 2004 (http://www.number-10.gov.uk/su/ethnicminorities/report/down loads/ethnic_minorities.pdf)

Kemp, R (1995) *An Apology in Ghana*, Essence, October

Kotkin, J (1996) The Global Power of Tribes: An Interview with Joel Kotkin, *Leader to Leader*, No. 2 Fall 1996, http://leadertoleader.org/leaderbooks/L2L/fall96/kotkin.html

Kotkins (1993) *Tribes of the 21st Century: How Race, Religion and Identity Determine Success in the New Global Economy,* New York: Random House

Kotre, J (2004) Generativity and Culture: What Meaning Can Do in *The Generative Society: Caring for Future Generations* (eds) E de St Aubin, D P McAdams and T Kim, American Psychological Association, Washington, DC

Kotre, J (1983) *Outliving the Self: How We Live On In Future Generations*, W W Norton and Company: New York and London

Krasko, G L (1997) Viktor Frankl: The Prophet of Meaning, http://www.meaning.ca/articles/featured article_archive.html, retrieved April 2006

Lacey, K R (2004) Black Spaces, Black Places: Strategic Assimilation and Identity Construction in Middle-Class Suburbia, *Ethnic and Racial Studies*, 27:6, pp908-930, DOI: 10.1080/014198704 2000268521

Laing, R D (1961) *Self and Others*, Penguin Books

Lawson, J (2003) The Wounds we Hide, The Other Side Online, (c) 2003 *The Other Side*, March-April 2003, Vol 39, No 2

LDA (2004) *The Educational Experiences and Achievements of Black Boys in London Schools,* 2000-2003: A Report by the Education Commission, http://www.lda.gov.uk/upload/pdf/ Educational_experiences.pdf

Leary, J D (2005) *Post Traumatic Slave Syndrome: America's Legacy of Enduring Injury and Healing,* Uptone Press

Leicester, M and Lovell, T (1994) Equal Opportunities and University Practice: Race, Gender and Disability: A Comparative Perspective in *Journal of Further and Higher Education,* 18(2)

Lincoln, C E (1995) *Black Religion and Racial Identity in Racial and Ethnic Identity: Psychological Development and Creative Expression* (ed) E E H Griffiths, H C Blue and H W Harris, Routledge

Lipsky, S (1987) *Internalised Racism,* Rational Island Publishers, USA

Lukes, S (1974) *Power: A Radical View,* MacMillan

Luz Reyes, M de la and Halcon, J J (1988) Racism in Academia: The Old Wolf Revisited, *Harvard Educational Review*, 58(3) pp299-314

Macpherson, W (1999) *The Stephen Lawrence Inquiry* Report of an Inquiry by Sir William Macpherson of Cluny, HMSO

MacTaggart, F (2004) http://www.ind.homeoffice.gov.uk/ind/en/home/news/archive/2004/august0/ commemorating_the.html

Madood, T (2004) *A Defence of Multiculturalism*, Lawrence and Wishart Independent Publishers, On-Line Articles, Issue 29, http://www.l-w-bks.co.uk/journals/articles/modood.html

Madood T (2002) *Ethnicity and intergenerational identities and adaptation in Britain*, paper given at the Jacobs Foundation Conference. Marbach Conference Centre (24-26 October, 2002)

Majors, R and Billson, J M (1992) *Cool Pose: The Dilemmas of Black Manhood in America*, New York: Lexington Books

Malik, K (1996) *The Meaning of Race: Race, History and Culture in Western Society*, Macmillan

Maltz, M (1960) *Psycho-Cybernetics*, Prentice-Hall Inc, USA

Mamon, S (2003) Crisis of Black Underachievement in London Schools, *IIR News*, http://www.irr.org.uk/2003/may/ak000015.html

Marcia, J. (1966) Development and validation of ego-identity status. *Journal of Personality and Social Psychology*, 3, 551-558

Marriot, D M (2003) Ending the Silence, *Kappan Professional Journal*, Phi Delta Kappa International

Martinas, S (1992) *The Culture of White Supremacy*, CWS Workshop. Web address http://www.prisonactivist.org/cws/cws-culture.html

Mashengele, D (1997) *Africentricity: New Context, New Challenges, New Futures*, 29th Annual SCUTREA Conference Proceedings, Crossing Borders, Breaking Boundaries: Research in the Education of Adults, Education-line, http://www.leeds.ac.uk/educol/docum,ents/000000261.htm

Matsuura, K (2004) Message from the director-general of UNESCO on the occasion of the International Year to Commemorate the Struggle Against Slavery and Its Abolition, UNESCO News Archives, Retrieved September 2004 from http://portal.unesco.org/en/ev.php-URI_ID=178048&URL_DO=DO_TOPIC&URL_SECTION=201.htm

Mazrui, A A (1990) *Cultural Forces in World Politics*, James Curry: London

McClean, C, Campbell, C and Cornish, F (2005) African-Caribbean interactions with mental health serves: experiences and expectations of exclusion as (re)productive of health inequalities, *LSE Research Online*, http//:eprints.lse.ac.uk/archive/00000180

McKellar, B (1989) Only the Fittest of the Fit Will Survive: Black Women and Education, *Women Teachers: Issues and Experiences* (ed) H De Lyon and F Widdowson, Migniuolo, OUP

McWhorter, J (2001) *Losing the Race: Self-Sabotage in Black America*, Perennial: New York

Midgette, T E and Meggert, S S (1991) Multicultural Counseling Instruction: A Challenge for Faculties in the 21st Century, *Journal of Counselling and Development*, Vol 70

Miller T and Yúdice G (2002) *Cultural Policy*, London: Sage

Moghissi, H (1994) Racism and Sexism in Academic Practice: A Case Study, *The Dynamics of 'Race' and Gender: Some Feminist Interventions*, H Afshar and M Maynard (eds), Taylor and Francis

Morgan, G (1986) *Images of Organisation*, Sage Publications

Morgan, G (1983) *Beyond Method: Strategies for Social Research*, Sage Publications Inc

Mukhopadhyay, C and Henze, R C (2003) Is Race Real: Using Anthropology to Make Sense of Human Diversity, *Kappan Professional Journal*

Myss, C (2002) *Sacred Contracts: Awakening Your Divine Potential*, Bantam Books, UK

Naipaul, V S (2002) *The Middle Passage*, Vintage: reprint edition

Newman, (2002) Socialisation, http://everything2.com/index.pl?node_id=100379

Ngugi, W T (1987) *Decolonising the Mind: The Politics of Language in African Literature*, James Curry

Nobles, W (1976) Black People in White Insanity: An Issue for Black Community Mental Health, *Journal of Afro-American Issues*, 4:1

Nobles, W (1985) *Africanity and the Black Family*, Black Family Institute Publications, Oakland

Ogbu, J U (1997) Understanding the School Performance of Urban African-Americans: Some Essential Background Knowledge. In H Walberg, O Reyes and R Weissberg (eds) *Children and Youth: Interdisciplinary Perspectives*, London: Sage

Ogbu, J U (1991) *Cultural Diversity and School Experience, Literary as Praxis: Culture, Language and Pedagogy,* (ed) Walsh, C E, Ablex Publishing Corporation

Okri, B (1997) *A Way of Being Free,* Phoenix

ONS (2003) *Ethnic Group Statistics A Guide for the Collection and Classification of Ethnic Data,* HMSO

Painter, N I (1995) *Soul Murder and Slavery, The Fifteenth Charles Edmondson Historical Lectures,* Baylor University, Waco: Texas: Markham Press Fund, 1995

Palmer, J A (2001) *Fifty major thinkers on education: from Confucius to Dewey,* Routledge, London and New York

Palmer, J A (2001) *Fifty modern thinkers on education: from Piaget to the present,* Routledge, London and New York

Palmer, P (1997) *The Courage to Teach: Exploring the Inner Landscape of a Teacher's Life,* San Francisco: Jossey-Bass Publishers

Palmer, P (1993) Good Talk About Good Teaching, *Change Magazine,* Vol. 25, Issue 6, pp. 8-13, Nov/Dec 1993. Published by Heldref Publications http://www.teacherformation.org/html/rr/divided-f.cfm

Palmer, P (1992) Divided No More: A Movement Approach to Educational Reform, *Change Magazine,* Vol. 24:2, pp.10-17, Mar/Apr 1992 http://www.mcli.dist.maricopa.edu/events/afc99/articles/divided.html

Parekh, B (2005) *Rethinking Multiculturalism: Cultural Diversity and Political Theory,* Palgrave Macmillan

Park, J (1999) *Becoming more authentic: the positive side of existentialism,* Minneapolis, MN: www.existentialbooks.com

Pascale, R (1991) *Managing on the Edge: How Successful Companies Use Conflict to Stay Ahead,* Penguin

Patterson, O (1982) *Slavery and Social Death: A Comparative Study,* Harvard University Press

Patterson, O (1973) *The Sociology of Slavery,* Granada Publishing Limited

Paxman, J (1999) *The English: A Portrait of a People,* Penguin Books Ltd; New Ed edition

Pettigrew, T F and Martin, J (1987) Shaping the Organisational Context for Black Americans, *Journal of Social Issues,* 43

Phillips, D and Berman, Y (2003) Social Quality and Ethnos Communities: Concepts and Indicators, *Community Development Journal* (38)4 October 2003, p344-357

Phinney, J, Lochner, B T and Murphy, R (1990) Ethnic Identity Development and Psychological Adjustment in Adolescence. In *Ethnic Issues in Adolescent Mental Health,* (eds) A R Stiffman and L E Davis, Sage Publications

Pinderhughes, E (1979) Afro-Americans and Economic Dependency, *The Urban and Social Change Review,* 12(2) 24-37

Proudford, K (1999) The Dynamics of Stigmatising Difference, *Journal of Career Development,* Vol 26:1, pp7-20, Springer Netherlands

Pryce, K (1979) *Endless Pressure,* Penguin Books Limited, England

Putnam, R (1993) Unlocking Organisational Routines that Prevent Learning, *The Systems Thinker: Building Shared Understanding,* 4(6), August Pegagus Communications Inc

Rao, A and Kelleher, D (2000) Leadership for Social Transformation: Some Ideas and Questions on Institutions and Feminist Leadership, *Gender and Development*, Vol 8 No 3

Reason P (2001) Learning and Change through action research in J Henry (ed) *Creative Management*, London: Sage

Reason, P. and Torbert, W. 2001. The action turn: Toward a transformational social science. *Concepts and Transformation*, 6:1, 1-37

Rex, J (1982) West Indian and Asian Youth in *Black Youth in Crisis,* (eds) Cashmore, E and Troyna, B, George Allen and Unwin, London

Richardson, N (2003) *'Why Racial Justice Matters for White Folks',* Racial Justice: Speak Truth to Power, Pendle Hill Monday Night Forum 2002-2003, Pendle Hill, 1930-2006

Richmond, A H (1954) *Colour prejudice in Britain: a study of West Indian workers in Liverpool, 1941-1951*, London, Routledge and Kegan Paul

Rinpoche, S (1992) *The Tibetan Book of Living and Dying*, Rider

Robb, W M (1997) Should the curriculum for educators of adults include a study of humanness? *Education-line*, http://www.leeds.ac.uk/educol/documents

Rodney, W (1989) *How Europe Underdeveloped Africa*, East African Educational Publishers

Samuel, M (1963) Little Did I Know: Recollections and Reflections, New York: Alfred A. Knopf, http://www.encyclopedia.com/doc/1G1-20583580.html

Sarkar, B (2001) Consciousness – Our Third Eye, Life Positive, September 2001, http://www.lifepositive.com/Mind/consciousness/human-consciousness.asp

Schafer, D P (2000) *Culture and cultures: Key Learning Requirements for the Future*, http://www.creatinglearningcommunities.org/book/additional/schafer.htm

Schein, E H (1988) *Process Consultation,* Addison-Wesley

SCMH (2002) An Executive Briefing on Breaking the Circles of Fear, *Briefing* 17, Sainsbury Centre for Mental Health

Segal, D (1995) *The Black Diaspora*, Faber and Faber

Seward, L G (2002) A Time for Inclusion: Strategies Encouraging the Success of All Students, *AAHE Bulletin,* March

Shengold, L (1989) *Soul Murder: The Effects of Childhood Abuse and Deprivation*, Fawcett Columbine, New York

Simon, R I (1992) *Teaching Against the Grain: Texts for a Pedagogy of Possibility*, Bergin and Garvey, USA

Simpson, L, Wood, L and Daws, L (2003) Community Capacity Building: Starting with People Not Projects, *Community Development Journal* (38)4 October 2003, p277-268

Sivanandan, A (1974) *Alien Gods, Colour, Culture and Consciousness: Immigrant Intellectuals in Britain,* (ed) B Parekh, George Allen and Unwin

Skillings, J H and Dobbins, J E (1991) Racism as a Disease: Etiology and Treatment Implications, *Journal of Counseling and Development*, volume 70

Skowron, E A (2004) Differentiation of self, personal adjustment, problem solving and ethnic group belonging amongst people of colour, *Journal of Counseling and Development,* Volume 82 pp337-456

Smith, D J (1976) The Facts of Racial Disadvantage: A National Survey, Volume XLII Broadsheet No 560, PEP: London

Smith, E J (1991) Ethnic Identity Development: Toward the Development of a Theory Within the Context of Majority/Minority Status, *Journal of Counseling and Development*, September-October, Vol.70

Solomos, R C (1993) *Race and Racism in Britain*, Macmillan, 2nd Edition

Some, M P (1994) *Of Water and the Spirit: Ritual, Magic and Initiation in the Life of an African Shaman*, Penguin

Spender, D (1982) *Women of Ideas (and what men have done to them)*, Ark Paperbacks

Spurgeon, C H (1866) *Soul Murder – Who is Guilty?* No. 713. Metropolitan Tabernacle, Newington. http://www.spurgeongems.org/vols10-12/chs713.pdf

St Aubin, E de (2004) The Propogation of Genes and Memes: Generativity Through Culture in Japan and the United States, in *The Generative Society: Caring for Future Generations*, E de St. Aubin, D P McAdams and T Kim (eds), American Psychological Association, Washington, DC

Stanton-Salazar, R D (1997) A Social Capital Framework for Understanding the Socialisation of Racial Minority Children and Youths, *Harvard Educational Review*, 67(1) pp1-40

Steele, S (1980) *The Content Of Our Character: A New Vision of Race in America*. St. Martin's Press: New York

Stone, H and Stone S (2000) *The Shadow King: The Invisible Force That Holds Women Back*, backinprint.com

Stonequist, E. V. (1961) *The marginal man: a study in personality and culture conflict*, New York: Russel and Russel, inc

Strauss, W and Howe, N (1991) *Generations: The History of America's Future, 1564 to 2069*, Quill William Morrow, New York

Sveiby, K I (1997) *Tacit Knowledge*, http://www.sveiby.com/articles/Polanyi.html

Swimme, B (1997) Science as Wisdom: The New Story as a Way Forward. An Interview with Lauren de Boer in *Adult Learning as a Hero's Journey: Researching Mythic Structure as a Model for Transformative Change*, J Simpson and P Coombes, http://www.iier.org.au/qjer/qjer17/ simpson. html

Tafarodi, R W, Kamg, S and Milne, A B (2002) When Different Becomes Similar: Compensatory Conformity in Bicultural Visible Minorities, *PSPB*, vol 28:8, pp1131-1142

Thernstrom, A and Thernstrom, S (2003) *No Excuses: Closing the Racial Gap in Learning*, Simon and Schuster Paperbacks

Thomas, D A (1989) Mentoring and Irrationality: The Role of Racial Taboos, *Human Resource Management*, (28)2 Summer, p279-290

Thomas, D A and Alderfer, C P (1989) The Influence of Race on Career Dynamics: Theory and Research on Minority Career Experiences in *Handbook of Career Theory*, (eds) M B Arthur, D T Hall and B S Lawrence, Cambridge University Press

Timimi, S B (1996) Race and Colour in Internal and External Reality, *British Journal of Psychotherapy*, 13(2), pp183-192

Torbert, W R (1991) *The Power of Balance: Transforming Self, Society and Scientific Inquiry*, Newbury Park, CA:Sage Publications

Torbert, W R and Fisher, D (1992) Autobiographical Awareness as a Catalyst for Managerial and Organisational Development, *Management Education and Development*, 23(3)184-198

Troyna, B (1987) *Racial Inequality in Education*, Routledge

Troyna, B (1988) *Afro-Caribbeans in the UK, Dictionary of Race and Ethnic Relations*, Routledge (ed) E Cashmore (2nd Edition)

Van Dijk, T A (1993) Elite Discourse and Racism, *Sage Series on Race and Ethnic Relations*, Volume 6

Vanzant, I (1993) *Acts of Faith: Daily Mediations for People of Colour,* Simon and Schuster

Vogler, C (1996) *The Writer's Journey: Mythic Structure for Storytellers and Screenwriters*, London: Boxtree

Watts-Jones, D (2002) *Healing Internalised Racism: The Role of a Within-Group Sanctuary Among People of African Descent*, Ackerman Institute for the Family, New York

Weick, K E (1995) *Sensemaking in Organisations*, Sage Publications

Whyte, D (1994) *The Heart Aroused: Poetry and the Preservation of the Soul at Work*, The Industrial Society

Widdowson, M (2001) *The Phoenix Principle and the Coming Dark Age*: Social Catastrophes – Human Progress 3000 BC to AD 3000, Amarna Ltd, Bedford, http://www.darkage.fsnet.co.uk/Book.htm

Williams, C (1987) *The Destruction of Black Civilisation: Great Issues of Race from 4500 BC to 2000 AD*, Third World Press

Wilson, A N (1993) *The Falsification of the Afrikan Consciousness: Eurocentric History, Psychiatry and the Politics of White Supremacy*, Afrikan World Info Systems, NY

Winton, K (2003) *On the Ethics of Exporting Ethics:* The Right to Silence in Japan and the U.S., John F Kennedy School of Government, Harvard University, Faculty Research Working Papers Series, http://ksgnotes1.harvard.edu/research/wpaper.nsf/rwp/rwp03.027

Wise, T (2004) *Personal Responsibility is a two-way street,* Znet Daily Commentaries, http://www.zmag.org/sustainers/content/2004-06/24wise.cfm

Young, C. (2000) Shadow on the heart: Soul murder and the destruction of the imagination. (Doctoral dissertation, Pacifica Graduate Institute). UMI no. 3029754. http://www.online.pacifica.edu/pgl/stories/storyReader$544

Index